Priesthood *for* all Believers

Priesthood *for* All Believers

Clericalism and How To Avoid It

Simon Cuff

scm press

© Simon Cuff 2022
Published in 2022 by SCM Press
Editorial office
3rd Floor, Invicta House,
108–114 Golden Lane,
London EC1Y 0TG, UK
www.scmpress.co.uk

SCM Press is an imprint of Hymns Ancient & Modern Ltd
(a registered charity)

Hymns Ancient & Modern® is a registered trademark of
Hymns Ancient & Modern Ltd
13A Hellesdon Park Road, Norwich,
Norfolk NR6 5DR, UK

British Library Cataloguing in Publication data
A catalogue record for this book is available
from the British Library

978-0-334-06102-1

Typeset by Regent Typesetting
Printed and bound by
CPI Group (UK) Ltd

For the people of God

The Church is defined by the acts of God
which create and sustain it, systems are defined
by the opinions held by their upholders: the
difference is a radical one.

Michael Ramsey[1]

1 Michael Ramsey, F. D. *Maurice and the Conflicts of Modern Theology* (Cambridge: Cambridge University Press, 1951), p. 33.

Contents

Acknowledgements

Once again, I owe a debt of thanks to all at SCM Press, and especially David Shervington for his continued guidance and support. This book was written at the end of my time at St Mellitus College as I prepared to be installed as Vicar of St Peter de Beauvoir Town. Thanks are due to the Bishop of Stepney and the parish representatives of St Peter de Beauvoir, whose generous appointment spurred me on in the final days of writing and who I hope will benefit from some of the ministry of priesthood and underlying theology of vocation that lies behind this text. Thanks are due to colleagues at St Mellitus who encouraged me in these ideas and whose conversation has fed into many of these themes, especially Selina Stone, Renie Choy, (Mthr) Cara Lovell, Joseph Diwakar, Emily Kempson, Mark Knight, Mthr Donna Lazenby, Jane Williams, Fr Michael Leyden, Alice Smith, Fr Lincoln Harvey, and Fr Russell Winfield. Fr Richard Springer also deserves special thanks for discussions on the theme of power and the necessity of a renewed priesthood to enable the capacity of all God's people to act. Thank you too for those who have challenged me in various contexts to think through my own relation to power, which lie behind some of the themes in Chapter 6, especially Zrinka Bralo, Amelia Viney, Charlotte Fischer and Marzena Cichon-Balcerowicz. This chapter all bears the fruit of some reflection offered to the Liturgical Commission of the Church of England. I began the final drafting of this book at the end of the third period of lockdown during the Coronavirus pandemic. The people of God gathered at St Cyprian's Clarence Gate were a constant source of inspiration and encouragement, especially Fr Michael Fuller to whom I owe a special debt for his enthusiastic support. The friendship of Mthr Sally Jones, Mthr Kristina Andréasson and Kyle Sawhney was a huge lift in the midst of lockdown. Thank you to Fr Jonathan Jong for commissioning an article on the 'secret' prayers of the Mass for St Mary Magdalen's School of Theology (www.theschoolof theology.org), some of which lies behind Chapter 4. I owe a special thanks to Deacon Jane Robinson's gentle and challenging ministry to the margins which convinced me of the importance of the vocation to the diaconate for the flourishing of the whole Church. This book is the fruit of some of my reflection on my own particular calling to ordained ministry in the Church of England. There are too many women and men of God to name who bear the responsibility for this vocation and my own poor attempt to live out the particular calling to ordained priesthood day by day. Thanks are owed to all those women and men of God who have shown me something of the particularity of Christian calling and the particular vocation to priesthood in which it is a daily privilege to serve, especially Jackie Ashmenall, and the incorrigible and Reverend Nev Boundy. Mthr Jenn Strawbridge, Fr Hugh Wybrew, Fr Andrew Davis, Fr Peter Groves, Br Philip SSF and others who showed me the gift of how the particular vocation to priesthood could be exercised in the catholic tradition of the Church of England in such a way as to enable the capacity to act of all those God is calling to serve. It is for all those people God is calling to their own particular vocation that this book is dedicated. As ever, this book would have been impossible without the constant support of Fr Jack Noble. All mistakes remain my own.

Simon Cuff
Feast of All Saints 2021

Introduction

Clericalism arises from an elitist and exclusivist vision of
vocation, that interprets the ministry received as a power to
be exercised rather than as a free and generous service to be
given. This leads us to believe that we belong to a group that
has all the answers and no longer needs to listen or learn anything, or that pretends to listen. Clericalism is a perversion
and is the root of many evils in the Church. (Pope Francis[1])

This is a book about clericalism. You might not think that
clericalism is the most exciting topic to read about or even
the most important in the Christian life. However, I want
to convince you that clericalism is something of which every
Christian needs to be aware because clericalism is everywhere,
and perhaps not where you might expect.

Clericalism, as we'll explore, is not just something to do
with clerics – the clergy or professional pastors and ministers.
Clericalism is the elevation of certain models, vocations or
ways of being Church in such a way as to diminish others.
Ironically, clericalism is bad for those who seemingly benefit
from it too – it can lead to their burn-out and a diminishing of
their vocation. Clericalism restricts the life of the Church and
individual Christians.

Knee-jerk reactions to overcome clericalism by clericalizing
lay people help no one. Popular phrases such as the 'priesthood
of all believers' run the risk of making all believers' vocations
squeeze into 'one size fits all' models of vocation and ministry,
in which vocation is robbed of its particularity. Again and again
throughout this book we shall see that *particularity* of vocation

and *intentionality* of living out vocation are central tools in the Church's toolbox to stop clericalism in its tracks. Some attempts to be less clericalist by doing away with certain forms of ministry can be more clericalist than the patterns they seek to replace – especially if they do away with the *particularity* of certain vocations. The irony here is that one of the best ways to overcome clericalism is a more intentional focus on particular ministries and the particular ministry of the ordained, not less. We shall see that part of the *particular* vocation of ordained ministers is to call all of us to pay particular attention and intention to our vocation – what it is we are called to be and to do. To overcome clericalism requires a better exercise of ordained ministry, not a lesser one. We shall see further that the tools which the ordained ministry – and ordained priesthood in particular – have inherited over centuries are a particular help in the daily life of every Christian. These tools we shall explore help us to keep our attention fixed on Christ, to cultivate an intentionality that is essential in Christian living, and to discover the particular calling that God has placed on our lives. This will be the particular focus of Chapter 5. Far from being a fringe topic of interest, clericalism and how we avoid it offers us a chance to focus on how to live the Christian life that builds up the whole body of Christ and helps us to play our part in allowing the vocation of those we live and serve alongside to flourish, whatever our calling.

Admittedly, although perhaps not something that Christians spend all that much time thinking about, 'clericalism' is a persistent danger in the Christian life. All too often we restrict our notion of 'clericalism' to clerics themselves. We fear the danger of 'clericalism' lies in too much power and influence in the Church being wielded by 'clerics'. The cleric we have in mind usually presides over churches and congregations whose worship and day-to-day life centres around the role of the priest or licensed pastor. In such clericalist churches, the preacher wields power with little or limited accountability as a divinely ordained agent of the Almighty. Mother or Father knows best.

The argument of this book is that while such forms of

'clericalism' are obviously anathema to the flourishing of each and every member of the body of Christ, 'clericalism' itself is a wider phenomenon than simply the undue and unchecked power of the clergy. In fact, to reduce 'clericalism' to the role of ordained clerics or appointed preachers is itself a form of 'clericalism' which can inhibit flourishing within the body of Christ. Such 'clericalism' seeks to avoid the danger of particularly noticeable forms of 'clericalism' exhibited by clergy. However, it does so at a greater cost – making the phenomenon of clericalism harder to see and therefore potentially more of a danger to the flourishing of each and every member of the body of Christ. The antidote to clericalism is not the hasty renunciation of clergy and particular forms of ministry. In fact, this book argues that ordained and particular ministries when modelled on Christ's priesthood are not inherently clericalist and, in fact, a potentially powerful antidote to some of the dangers inherent in clericalism. A focus on the precise nature of Christ's priesthood as an antidote to clericalism will be our focus in Chapter 2, and we will consider how this priesthood relates to the 'priesthood of all believers' in Chapter 4. Throughout, we shall argue that the model of power and leadership ordained ministry can inspire is an important witness to the wider world on how the particular flourishing of each and every individual can be enabled through the manner in which power is held across communities and peoples, and how as individuals we can serve the genuine flourishing of all those around us. In short, ordained ministry contributes to the flourishing of the whole when it is an exercise in radical solidarity – a solidarity from which the world can learn and which it sorely needs.

Therefore, while this is a book about the particular affront to solidarity that is clericalism, it is also a book about ordained ministry generally and priesthood in particular. In what follows I will tend to refer to the ordained priesthood primarily as it is the particular form of ordained ministry to which I have been called and confirmed in that calling through the ministry of the Church of England. This priesthood is the particular vocation I have been allotted to enable the particular vocation and flourishing of all those I serve and with whom I interact. Unless explicitly stated, much of what will be said will be transferable to other forms of ordained ministry: ordained deacons and bishops. With one caveat: from experience and because of the manner in which the Church of England and other denominations are currently ordered, those ordained and exercising the ministry of 'distinctive' or 'permanent' deacons are perhaps less likely to run the risk of some of the dangers of clericalism described in this book. We shall explore how the priestliness of the diaconal ministry is itself a powerful antidote to clericalism. The experience of deacons in the world and alongside those marginalized by the Church and world enables a keener sense of the patterns of clericalism we will encounter below. Indeed, when ordained ministry is truly 'anti-clericalist' it resides in and reflects the very margins with which the ministry of the deacon is associated. For now, I will resist the temptation to suggest whether those who exercise the ministry of bishop or overseer are more or less likely to be in danger of falling foul of the phenomenon of clericalism.

This book is written from the perspective of an ordained priest within a particular denominational tradition (the catholic tradition of the Church of England) and is an exercise in reflection on the potential gifts of this particular lived tradition for the overcoming of clericalism in all traditions. It is an attempt to develop and articulate a lived doctrine of Christian priesthood and ordained and particular ministries, which is both 'anti-clericalist' and also enables sharing the gifts of ordained and licensed ministries in enabling the flourishing of the entire people of God. The use of the term 'anti-clericalist' deliberately echoes the term 'anti-racist'. To inhabit the advantages of an ordained priesthood in enabling the flourishing of the lived priesthood of each and every member of the body of Christ requires the same posture of intentionality that the struggle for racial justice has taught us is required to develop a truly anti-racist society and Church. We shall see how the exercise of ordained ministry in such a way can learn from and is a tool towards the kind of anti-racist and anti-discriminatory Church for which we all long. In short: to inhabit one's calling and flourishing in a way that does not inhibit others' callings, but rather enables their flourishing, and yours, through this radical solidarity.

Central to our argument is the recognition that while the ordained priesthood and the elevation or licensing of particular ministries runs the risk of 'clericalism', it is not avoided by removing or simply shifting focus away from the ordination or licensing of particular individuals for particular ministries. In fact, this can make the danger of 'clericalism' considerably worse. Instead, we will argue, when inhabited intentionally and aware of the dangers of clericalism, the ordained priesthood and particularity of ministries are some of the best means of overcoming clericalism. Ordained priesthood, as we shall see, exists only to enable the flourishing of the entirety of the priestly body of Christ. An ordained priesthood, exercised by those who are called to this *particular* way of Christian life and witness, will enable the flourishing of all those who are called to other *particular* forms of ministry and Christian life.

Such priesthood points to the way in which all of us can live out Christian calling so that it is truly 'anti-clericalist' and overcomes the dangers inherent in clericalism. The litmus test of ordained priesthood and ministry becomes the extent to which it enables the flourishing of the 'priesthood' of each and every member of the body of Christ. That is, the extent to which it enables the living out of the *particular* calling to flourishing of each and every member of the body of Christ.

There is the potential that this book could be another in a long line of books about 'priesthood', usually read by those in or exploring or discerning vocation to ordained ministry. There are many, many excellent and faithful priests in God's Church. There are almost as many books on the subject of priesthood. However, there are far fewer excellent books on priesthood than there are excellent priests and ordained ministry. There are a number of reasons that it is difficult to write good books on the ministry of these excellent and faithful priests. First, it's quite hard to put into words the ministry of priesthood. There is something rightly described as mysterious about ordained ministry. There is a divine 'given-ness' to priesthood that's hard to explain. It is a ministry of 'being there' which at one level is no different from other particular Christian ministries and callings but is also utterly different and peculiarly distinct. Trying to put into words this complete sameness to, and utter difference from, other Christian ministries is very nearly impossible. This accounts for why so many books on Christian priesthood sometimes feel like they miss the mark.

Second, books on priesthood also tend to be written for those ordained priests to nurture or sustain them in their ministry or for those exploring a call to ordained ministry. This means that they rightly tend to focus on the ministry of the ordained priesthood. However, such a focus on the ordained priesthood often means that such priestly books end up describing the ordained priesthood in an ironically unpriestly way. That is, through a necessary focus on priestly ministry they unintentionally contribute to the phenomenon of clericalism rather than enable Christian ministry to overcome it. As we shall see, the ordained priesthood, and ordained priests, are not really meant to be the focus. Rather, ordained priesthood exists to perpetually refocus the body of Christ not on the ordained priesthood itself but on Christ – from whose primary priesthood all Christian ministry derives – and from those currently marginalized from the practices and processes of the Church and world.

This focus on priesthood may well open the author to the charge of 'clericalism'. This book is therefore an attempt to write a book on priesthood that is deliberately priestly in a properly priestly way. That is, it sets out to model (albeit in an inevitably flawed way) how to exercise the particular vocation of this author – to ordained priesthood – in a way that is decidedly anti-clericalist. To some extent it therefore flows out of the priestly vocation of the author. We shall see below that an essential part of priestliness is to exist to point away from oneself and towards Christ, and to help remove the stumbling blocks that can get in the way of Christians in their relationship to Christ and their flourishing in their calling and vocation. There are very many such stumbling blocks that get in the way of an individual or community's flourishing and relationship with Christ: sin, idolatry, racism, misogyny, trans- and homophobia, and more besides. It's important to note from the outset what will become a focus of this book – that clericalism, an undue focus on particular ministries or even the ordained priesthood itself, constitutes in itself such a stumbling block.

The vocation of ordained ministry includes clearing the way of such stumbling blocks of which the stumbling block of clericalism is perhaps always the most difficult to address, because the inevitable tendency is for the Church to try to address clericalism in a clericalist way.

The extent of clericalism

Before we go any further it's helpful to pause to reflect on what precisely we mean by clericalism. It's helpful here to look at Pope Francis' recent articulation of the concept of clericalism to help us appreciate the potential breadth of this phenomenon. He has described clericalism as 'one of the strongest and most serious dangers in the Church today'.[2]

Pope Francis describes clericalism as a distortion which 'nullifies the character of Christians, but also tends to diminish and undervalue the baptismal grace that the Holy Spirit has placed in the heart of our people'.[3] Ironically, he suggests that clericalism robs the Church of the particularity of vocation through the 'homologization of the laity ... far from giving impetus to various contributions and proposals, gradually extinguishes the prophetic flame to which the entire Church is called to bear witness'.[4]

A Church that is affected by clericalism is a Church that has lost the diversity of gifts and recognition of the particular ministries of the entire people of God. Like a fizzy drink that has gone flat, the Church that is affected by clericalism loses its vibrancy and prophetic fizz. Clericalism, Pope Francis continues, 'forgets that the visibility and sacramentality of the Church belong to all the People of God, not only to the few chosen and enlightened'.[5] Here we begin to see how clericalism is a potential threat to the Church beyond simply the clericalism of the clergy. Any forms of ministry or groups of people who see themselves as especially chosen or enlightened above the entirety of the people of God represent a form of clericalism.

Elsewhere, Pope Francis uses the language of entitlement to describe this setting up of some over all: a 'sense of entitlement is the cancer of clericalism ... a perversion of the vocation to which we priests are called'.[6] The root sin of this sense of entitlement with respect to others is 'the sin of failing to respect the value of a person'.[7] Clericalism here is a misplaced emphasis which can lead to the abuse and devaluing of others through a focus on the perceived entitlement that a particular role or ministry brings at the expense of the proper exercise of that role or ministry for the sake of the flourishing and valuing of others. Here clericalism is not a result of ordained priesthood *per se* but a corruption of it, either through the way in which such ministry is exercised or because of the undue focus on the ministry of the ordained at the expense of the ministry and value of others.[8]

Indeed, this form of clericalism is also not limited to the ordained. Pope Francis again notes it is a kind of clericalism that creates new forms of lay 'elites' over and above a recognition of the particularity of varying ministries to which each and every Christian is called.[9] A recent debate within the Church of England helps us to understand Pope Francis' observation here.

In the summer of 2021, John McGinley sparked debate by implying in a presentation that – because of cost of training and sustaining – ordained ministry was a 'limiting factor' within growing Christian community in the Church of England.[10] His remarks were widely debated and hotly contested. However, for our purposes, it's not so much the optionality of ordained ministry to Christian community that his comments implied, but the context in which they were made which illustrates Pope

INTRODUCTION

Francis' observation. McGinley was speaking at the launch of a vision for the Church of England to establish 10,000 new 'lay-led' churches. This vision, with its focus on lay *leadership*, runs the risk of clericalizing such a lay-elite, rather than radically enabling the particular ministry of each Christian in a place (those called to lay ministry as much as those called to ordained ministry). We run the risk of clericalism where models of ordained leadership are simply taken over by those who are not ordained to produce a new form of clericalism and elite. In fact, as we have hinted above, the potential for clericalism here is greater as one of the functions of ordained life is to recall each particular calling to life to enable greater flourishing in vocation.

At root, clericalism is a form of improper inhabiting of power. It enables the flourishing and capacity to act of a particular part of the body of Christ at the expense of the flourishing of the entirety of the body of Christ. Here is the supreme irony. In those Christian traditions that operate an ordained priesthood, the ministry of the ordained is intended precisely to stop this process of clericalism. The ordained are set apart not to stultify other ministries but to enable them. The particularity of the ordained and the restriction of certain acts, such as the celebration of the Eucharist or the celebration and realization of absolution from sin (acts that belong properly to the whole body of Christ), are achieved by God through the *particular* exercise of ministry of *particular* people whose *particular* divinely gifted vocation is discerned by the Church in order to demonstrate the scandalous particularity of all vocation. The particularity of the vocation of the ordained, properly exercised, does not diminish capacity through the restriction of particular acts, but establishes the capacity and particularity of others in their vocation – or, at least, it should. This particularity of ministry is grounded above all in the scandalous particularity of Christ, God's incarnation as *one* of us – Jesus Christ the particular human being God became and in whom all vocations have their foundation and find their realization.

9

The inhibiting of the range of vocations and particular ways the particular people of God are being called to live the Christian life is one of the worst side effects of clericalism. It is analogous to the reduction in biodiversity in an ecosystem through climate change and limits the thriving of the whole people of God – including those whose clericalism has led to the restriction of the people of God in this way. We need to be careful here. Sometimes clericalism can be pursued for the best of intentions. The clericalism that leads to the creation of a new kind of lay elite can arise from the best of intentions. The good intention to enable the capacity of every person to exercise leadership in the Church becomes the clericalist reality of investment in lay forms of leadership which are not shaped according to the particular vocation of the individuals and communities in question, but according to the agenda of clergy and others who are sure they know the shape ministry *should* take. This robs the ministry of the lay 'elite' of the particularity of vocation and also diminishes the capacity of others – lay and ordained – to exercise the particular vocations to which they are being called.

Pope Francis recognizes the inclination to exercise power behind such clericalism. Clericalism fails to recognize that the creation of such lay elites is in fact the product of clericalism because clericalism is 'more concerned with dominating spaces'.[11] He recognizes that such views of ministry see vocation 'as a power to be exercised rather than as a free and generous service to be given. This leads us to believe that we belong to a group that has all the answers and no longer needs to listen or learn anything, or that pretends to listen.'[12] Once again we see how the potential for clericalism extends beyond the ordained. Any group or initiative within the Church that believes that it has all the answers and in effect franchises a model of growth or church revitalization runs the risk of clericalism. It does so because it runs the risk of imitating other individuals' or community's vocations rather than seeking to tenable the particularity of vocation to which God is calling the individual or community in question.

A Church that is radically anti-clericalist exercises all forms of ministry with radical solidarity to the individuals and communities by which it is constituted and which it exists to serve. This means rather than replicating models or franchises of revitalization, anti-clericalist ministry recognizes that there is the need for as many shapes of vocation as there are people in the body of Christ. This does not, however, do away with the particular vocation of the ordained, but rather is precisely that vocation. The ordained exist to serve and enable these vocations. In order to do so the ministry of the ordained must reflect and be sustained by the variety of particularity of those called into ministry.

Ordained ministry as prophetic particularity

In order to develop an anti-clericalist account of ordained ministry, we need to spend some time thinking about what it means to be ordained. We shall see below, in Chapter 3, that one attempt to address the danger of clericalism is to prioritize the notion of the 'priesthood of all believers'. However, all too often this focus on the 'priesthood of all believers' can end up having precisely the opposite outcome from what is intended. Clericalizing the entire body of Christ may offer less of a solution to the problem of removing this particular stumbling block to the Christian life than at first thought.

Instead, this book seeks to explore the role of the ordained priesthood as a means of reflecting on the entirety of the Christian life. It does so in the belief that one manner of exercising such a ministry in a way that enables rather than diminishes the vocation of others is by keeping one question constantly at the fore: 'What is the point of a priest?' This is a question that has been asked countless times in the history of the Church. It has been uttered with rage by kings and earthly rulers, with frustration by vexed bishops and church elders, with exasperation in parish meetings and by church members, in trembling uncertainty of themselves by members of the clergy.

What is the point of a priest? This book seeks to explore this question for Christians seeking to understand why it is that God has called particular individuals to particular priestly ministries in God's Church. It also seeks to help those who are exploring a call to priestly ministry or who are already exercising it to draw on the wisdom of earlier reflectors on the nature of Christian priesthood. It includes tools that earlier generations of Christians have passed down to us for the better exercise of priestly ministry. As such it aims both to nourish the priesthood of those of us who have been called to the ministry of priest and those who are exercising any Christian ministry by virtue of their baptismal calling which grants them their share in the priesthood of Christ or the 'priesthood of all believers' as it is sometimes known. Indeed, we shall see again and again that perhaps the only point of priests is to enable the priesthood of all believers. The priesthood of priests looks beyond itself for the flourishing of the priesthood of all believers, to better allow the whole body of Christ to share in the whole priesthood of Christ. Priests exist so that all of us may share better in the priesthood that is ours through baptism.

If priests are living up to their calling, priesthood is best understood as a ministry whose primary aim is to get out of the way. More often than not, this means helping those to whom we are sent and whom we are called to serve to get rid of the obstacles that get in the way of their relationship with Christ, and then to get out of the way ourselves. One of the perennial problems in the exercise of priestly ministry is that we begin helping those around us to clear obstacles to the exercise of their share in the priesthood of Christ, only to put new obstacles in their way by our frail exercising of priestly ministry. This is often due to the obstacle known as clericalism. Instead of clergy existing to liberate others to their particular calling, the particular calling of clergy is lived in such a way as to stifle the calling of others. Think of the subtitle of this book: 'clericalism and how to avoid it'. It needs to be said from the outset that it's wrong to think that clericalism is only a problem for traditions that have a defined set of roles and signs for the ministry of the ordained. The exercise of any Christian ministry is prone to being exercised in a 'clericalist' way, as we shall see.

These two themes – the priesthood of all believers and the perennial danger of clericalism – lead many to the view that the ordained ministry of clergy should be done away with altogether. The particular ministries of deacon, bishop and, more commonly, priest should be dispensed with as a misguided hangover from the ancient world or the medieval Church. This is not the argument of this book which seeks to recover God's intention for calling Christian denominations to order particular ministries in the way that has been received. We shall find that rather than the existence of ordained clergy leading inexorably to clericalism, the existence of ordained clergy is intended to save us from the clericalism and corresponding abuses of power. Just because the Church has failed in its vocation to exercise the particular priesthood of priests in such a way as to enable the priesthood of all believers is not an argument for the abolition of that priesthood altogether. In fact, the tools that have been bequeathed us through past generations who have found wisdom in the priestly ordering of the Church are the very tools needed to enable the particular priesthood of priest to serve its sacred calling so that all might be enabled to serve their sacred calling.

How does ordained ministry generally and the priesthood in particular help to save us from the ever-present danger of clericalism? Here I want us to think in broad terms about why ordained ministry in general – and the priesthood in particular – exists at all. In the next chapter, we will argue that as all priesthood is grounded in Christ's priesthood, we need to pay particular attention to the unlikeliness of Christ's priesthood. This unlikeliness prevents us from taking for granted the power or status in the exercise of priesthood and other ministries which might enable clericalism to take root. The sheer unlikeliness of Christ's priesthood forces the Church to look at who and how it discerns who is called to ordained ministry, and the processes by which they are ordained.

We've already hinted at the fact that trying to explore what the ordained ministry is and how and why it differs from other forms of ministry is not a simple task. There is a 'there-ness' and 'given-ness' to ordained ministry that mirrors the given-ness of all vocation and is not all that easy to explain. Rowan Williams, in an article that argued for the necessity of women's ordination at the height of debates in the Church of England, reflects both on this intangibility and on the necessity of priesthood – and a particular way of conceiving the priesthood – as a means for the Church to be what it is that God is calling into being. He writes:

> the institutionalizing of ministry (like the formation of the canon of Scripture) has, from very early on, been a vital part of that historical self-awareness which (in an ideal world!) should serve or empower the authority of believing women and men, and deliver them from the tyrannies of individual feeling and unspoken, unchecked manipulation (by me or by others), and in this sense is clearly pastoral as well as prophetic.[13]

For Williams, the function of ordained ministry is to empower believing women and men. That is, institutionalized or ordained ministry is intended to act against the mechanism of clericalism that disempowers the whole body of Christ by seemingly empowering a particular section or elite. The role of ordained ministry, according to Williams, is to enable the entire Church to remember that the Christian life is inevitably a calling, and to enable the entire Church to live out that calling more faithfully: 'the "apostolate" is a ministry representing the fact that the Church is *called*, and is answerable for its fidelity to this call ... the ordained – i.e. the "ordered", recognized, legitimized – ministry is there, most simply, to minister to the Church's very identity'.[14] Ordained ministry exists as a means to enable the faithfulness of every Christian – lay and ordained – to their particular calling.

Williams places a large caveat on the ability of the ordained to perform this role. He argues that in order for the ordained ministry to function as intended, to enable the entire body of Christ to flourish, it must be in solidarity with every member:

> Ordained ministry is there to address the unfulfilment and unconvertedness of the Church, to speak to the Church in the name of the Kingdom. It needs therefore to speak to the Church on behalf of the poor and excluded – and specifically of those whom the Church itself *causes* to be 'poor and excluded', to feel devalued, rejected or dehumanized. Can this be done with any credibility if the ordained ministry expresses no solidarity with such people? And these are questions not only about women, or homosexuals, or divorcees, but about all whose history is marked down by the Church as failure, whose experience is sealed off from the exercise of 'professional' pastoring. This, if anything, is the way to make pastoral ministry dramatically unprophetic.[15]

Ordained ministry, if it is to fulfil its prophetic role, cannot be sealed off from those the Church has previously excluded. These are precisely those whose former acts of clericalism have diminished the capacity to be that which God is calling them to be and the vocation God is calling them to exercise for the sake of the flourishing of the whole Church. However, this is not to say that *every* person is called to or should be ordained. To do so would itself be clericalist. Instead, the ordained ministry must show itself to be in solidarity with every member of the body of Christ – lay and ordained. This solidarity is risky, as Williams himself notes. He uses the example of predominantly middle-class clergy living in solidarity with the urban, inner city and estate communities that they serve: 'there is plenty of impressive solidarity in action, but, in the nature of the case, it rarely grows directly out of shared experience and common social interest. The priest is still someone who has *chosen* to identify.'[16] For such a priesthood to become anti-clericalist, it is necessary that the solidarity of priesthood be not just intentional but incidental – through the selection and ordination of those among whom a primarily middle-class clergy formerly ministered.

Such solidarity is not merely representation. The danger of a solely representative priesthood is that it is particularly susceptible to clericalism. The temptation for a particular ruling class or elite to ordain and highlight individuals from particular backgrounds as representatives of those backgrounds as a whole is open to the abuse of clericalism. The representatives are instrumentalized as symbols of the whole and the particular calling that God has in mind is made to take second place to the representative role they are ordained to serve. Again, the solution to this is ever constant vigilance: the ordained ministry must be alive to God's call to ordination among all those God is calling to ordination and each and every ministry of the Church.

The lot of the ordained

The particularity of vocation is hinted at even in the word 'clericalism'. We can conclude our introduction by reflecting on the particularity revealed in its etymology, as this particularity will be the foundation of the argument of this book. This particularity of calling is grounded in the particular person of Christ as the foundation of all ministry and is the subject of our next chapter.

The term derives from 'cleric' and is related to 'clergy'. Both these terms ultimately arrive into modern English through the Latin *clericus* or 'clerk'. Ordained ministers in the Church of England are sometimes referred to as 'Clerks in Holy Orders'. This qualification alerts us to the fact that there is nothing in the term 'clerk' itself that reduces it to ordination. There can be lay clerks in addition to the other forms of clerk, such as a legal clerk. The term 'clergy' in modern usage is almost universally exclusively applied to the ordained. However, the '*cler-*' of both 'clergy' and 'clerk' derive from the underlying Greek *klêros*, meaning 'lot' or 'that which is allotted'. Its connection with ministry is established in the Greek translation of the Old Testament with its use for that which is 'allotted' to the Levites from the tithes of Israel (Numbers 18.21). The term is used at the site of the crucifixion where those who crucified him cast 'lots' for Jesus' clothes. It's used in a more technical sense in Acts 1 for the election of Matthias over Justus to replace Judas in the ministry of the apostles – a passage that we will turn to shortly. Elsewhere in the New Testament, it's used in the sense of those who have been allotted by God to share in the Christian faith (Acts 26.18; Colossians 1.12) and also in the sense of those who have been allotted by God to the ministry of particular ministers. In 1 Peter we read of the importance of those exercising the ministry of 'presbyter' and 'overseer' are to do so towards those they have been allowed to serve, not lording it over them but as an example to the entire flock (1 Peter 5.3).

There is nothing in the term that limits 'that which is allotted' solely to the ordained. The lay person as much as the ordained are subject to this or that particular lot. The part of this etymology that is significant for us is the particularity of that which is allotted. God is calling you not to a general ministry and service but a particular one, the one that has been allotted to you by God. It's important to note the Church's role here in discerning and confirming with you that which God has allotted, which is where the episode in Acts 1 is so important for the themes of this book. This particularity of God's call – and its preparation in eternity – is a persistent theme of Scripture. Think of Paul's reflection on his vocation in Galatians 1.15: 'God, who had set me apart before I was born and called me through his grace.'

It might be tempting to argue for a return to a more general sense of the term 'clerk' over and above its contemporary restriction to the ordained in order to restore this sense of divine particularity and appointment not just to ordained callings but to all calling and Christian vocation. Licensed lay ministers within the Church of England – and others besides – are as much clerks in this sense as the ordained, and the use of the term 'licensed lay clerks' might help towards greater parity of esteem between ordained and lay ministry in the Church of England. However, as we shall see below, I suspect this would only lead to a further clericalizing of such roles rather than a radical liberation to exercise the particular calling for which God has set each of us apart. In what follows, we do not directly address the question of licensed lay ministries. However, the concept of particularity of vocation and the inhabiting of particular vocation in such a way that individuals flourish and enable others to flourish will be true of the variety of lay *and* ordained vocations and ministries. The focus we set out – on the radical particularity of ministry, the primacy of Christ's priesthood, the importance of overcoming processes of marginalization – will liberate lay ministries as much as ordained to fulfil their particular calling and to play their calling in contributing to the flourishing of those around them. In the case of licensed lay ministers, this will especially be felt in recognizing the particular vocation of the licensed lay minister as a prophetic minister of the word rather than a ministry which, like the ministry of deacons, is often defined only in contradistinction to the ministry of those ordained priest.

The use of the term *kleros* in Acts 1 and 8 offers important episodes for us on which to reflect, as they reveal much about this radical particularity of Christian calling and ministry. Acts 1 recounts the election of Matthias over Justus (also known as 'Joseph called Barsabbas'). The role of the *kleros* or 'lot' in this episode is widely known in the Christian imagination. The eleven apostles discern two candidates to replace Judas and cast 'lots' to decide which of the two it will be. The lot falls on Matthias and Justus is not allotted a place among the twelve. It's clear that Matthias has been allotted to a particular ministry and he takes his place among the twelve. However, this reading misses that Justus no less than Matthias has a particular vocation. His lot may not be among the twelve but that does not mean God has not allotted him a particular calling and share in Christian ministry. Tradition has it in fact that he goes on to be called to serve as bishop.

There is another 'lot' in Acts 1. As the story is framed in

Acts, the problem posed by Judas' betrayal makes reference too to Judas' allotted ministry. 'He was numbered among us and was allotted his share in this ministry' (Acts 1.17). Matthias' particular ministry among the twelve is framed as a taking up of the particular pattern of ministry to which Judas was called but which he had left behind (Acts 1.25). It's not just Matthias upon whom 'lots' fell, but each of the characters in this episode – Matthias, Justus and Judas – each has a particular ministry allotted to him. In these terms, Judas' turning aside following his betrayal may be seen in terms of the particular ministry allotted to him.

Acts 8 also makes use of the term and again the personal nature of this particularity is underscored. Just as both Matthias and Justus have particular ministries allowed to them, so it is with the former magician Simon. He sees the apostles conferring the gift of the Holy Spirit through the laying on of hands (Acts 8.17–18, which in church life continues today through laying on of hands in the sacrament of Confirmation), and he tries to buy this gift. He wants to serve in this particular ministry. Peter is typically harsh in his rebuke while responding to this request: 'May your silver perish with you, because you thought you could obtain God's gift with money! You have no part or share in this' (Acts 8.20–21). The word translated 'share' here is *kleros*. Peter tells Simon this is not the ministry to which he has been allotted. You cannot buy your way into a particular ministry which God has not allotted you. We might imagine the scene today at which a person is impressed by the bishop's ability to confirm candidates in a Confirmation service, so we ask her politely after the service how much it will cost to be able to share in the particular ministry of the episcopate to which she has been called. You cannot buy a calling which is not your own and to which you have not been allotted or called by God.

We might think the idea of offering a bishop cash after a Confirmation service is pretty unlikely to happen today. However, we should not be too quick to dismiss the reality that those with wealth, independent means or access to finance and influence – while perhaps not as brazen as Simon in their request to be granted a share in a particular ministry – all too often find it easier to access and thrive in church life today. While they might not be offering cash, the power, privilege and opportunity afforded them by their means all too often results in the Church being more ready to recognize and discern callings to particular ministries such as bishop over those who might be called to such ministries yet lack the finance, resources or influence to make themselves known. While Simon's example in Acts 8 underlines the particularity of ministry and reminds us we cannot buy ourselves into a particular ministry that God is not calling us towards, it also reminds us of the importance of discerning the call to particular ministries among those who lack the finance and means to make themselves known and who the Church might otherwise overlook. The privilege of the wealthy and influential as a particularly powerful elite is itself a form of clericalism. The voice of those with means is heard more loudly than those who lack the means to make their calling known throughout the Church. This prioritizing of the powerful is but one of the dangers of clericalism, and is perhaps one of the most serious.

It's time to turn now to the task of this book. We now move to consider how the unlikeliness of Christ's priesthood helps us to free all forms of ordained ministry, and particularly priesthood, from the scourge of clericalism. This requires us to put aside certain stereotypes of how Christ functions as priest, and to pay particular attention to the way in which Christ's priesthood in fact unfolds. This dual posture of attentiveness and leaving aside stereotypes will be essential to the achievement of this book's task. Pope Francis' words to a synod of bishops are apt for our task as much as they were for that meeting and for every assembly of God's assembly which is the Church:

It is therefore necessary, on the one hand, to decisively overcome the scourge of clericalism. Listening and leaving aside stereotypes are powerful antidotes to the risk of clericalism, to which an assembly such as this is inevitably exposed,

despite our intentions ... we must humbly ask forgiveness
for this and above all create the conditions so that it is not
repeated.[17]

Notes

1 Pope Francis, 'Opening of the XV Ordinary General Assembly
of the Synod of Bishops – Address by His Holiness Pope Francis at
the Opening of the Synod of Bishops on Young People, the Faith and
Vocational Discernment' (3 October 2018), available at: www.vatican.
va/content/francesco/en/speeches/2018/october/documents/papa-fran
cesco_20181003_apertura-sinodo.html [accessed 15.08.2021].

2 Pope Francis, 'Address to Participants in the General Chapter of
the Order of Clericals Regular of Somasca' (30 March 2017), available at: www.vatican.va/content/francesco/en/speeches/2017/march/
documents/papa-francesco_20170330_capitolo-chierici-somaschi.html
[accessed 16.08.2021].

3 Pope Francis, 'Letter to Cardinal Marc Ouellet President of the
Pontifical Commission for Latin America' (16 March 2016), available at: www.vatican.va/content/francesco/en/letters/2016/documents/
papa-francesco_20160319_pont-comm-america-latina.html [accessed
16.08.2021].

4 Pope Francis, 'Letter to Cardinal Ouellet'.

5 Pope Francis, 'Letter to Cardinal Ouellet'.

6 Pope Francis, *Let Us Dream: The Path to a Better Future* (London:
Simon & Schuster, 2020), p. 25.

7 Pope Francis, *Let Us Dream*, p. 25.

8 Pope Francis, *Let Us Dream*, p. 28.

9 Pope Francis, 'Letter to Cardinal Ouellet'.

10 See, for example, 'Leader Comment: "Key Limiting Factors"' (9
July 2021), available at: www.churchtimes.co.uk/articles/2021/9-july/
comment/leader-comment/leader-comment-key-limiting-factors
[accessed 8.09.2021].

11 Pope Francis, 'Letter to Cardinal Ouellet'.

12 Pope Francis, 'Opening of the XV Ordinary General Assembly'.

13 Rowan Williams, 'Women and the Ministry: A Case for Theological Seriousness' in Monica Furlong (ed.), *Feminine in the Church*
(London: SPCK, 1984), pp. 11–24 (p. 15).

14 Williams, 'Women and the Ministry', p. 15.

15 Williams, 'Women and the Ministry', pp. 23–4.

16 Williams, 'Women and the Ministry', p. 17.

17 Pope Francis, 'Opening of the XV Ordinary General Assembly'.

I

Christ's Unlikely Priesthood

If the ordained minister is not to be reduced to the level of a professional manager or administrator or even just a delegate of the Christian congregation, we need a firmer grounding of our theological vision in our understanding of the person of Christ. If Christ exercises no control on our theologising, then we had better admit that we have abandoned any attempt at continuity with mainstream Christian tradition. (Rowan Williams[1])

It's never a bad idea to begin theological thinking by reflecting on Jesus. In this chapter we seek to explore how ordained ministry generally and priesthood in particular might be exercised in an anti-clericalist way, through reflecting on the example of Christ's priesthood. The phrase 'Christ's priesthood' should immediately cause us to sit up and stop our theological thinking in its tracks. However, we are so used to thinking of Christ as the priest (one of three titles: Prophet, Priest and King) that we often draw lines from Christ's priesthood to the ordained priesthood or priesthood of all believers without spending a lot of time thinking precisely how it is that Christ is priest. Indeed, we rob Christ's priesthood of something of its unlikeliness by making Christ's priesthood foundational without pursuing our precise understanding of what it means for Christ to be priest.

This is not to say that Christ's priesthood is not foundational for all priesthood, indeed all forms of ordained ministry. Rather, for Christ's priesthood to be regarded as foundational in a way that liberates us from clericalist patterns and ways of holding office and power, rather than confirming and establishing them, we must constantly focus our attention on the way that Christ is priest. Doing so will perpetually surprise and upset our notions of priesthood in such a way as to refocus the manner in which we inhabit and discern vocation. The unlikeliness of Christ's priesthood enables us to keep God's search for the unlikely and the unexpected consistently at the fore. This is one of the surest guards against the 'likely' or the 'expected' or the 'entitled' gaining a foothold in our ways of being and existing as Church.

There is a danger in how we think about and live ordained ministry or those particular ministries we saw are liable to be elevated through the dynamics of clericalism. This danger stems from a lack of attention to the particularity of Christ's priesthood. All too easily Christ's priesthood is seen simply as a continuation par excellence or culmination of the cultic priesthood of Jesus' day. Jesus is seen as the best or sole example of priesthood and his priesthood is viewed as the example to which all other forms of priesthood relate. However, viewing Jesus' priesthood this way opens the door to a kind of clericalism of looking at priesthood simply as the domain of a priestly elite.

Looking at Jesus' priesthood this way finds its basis in Hebrews 7, a vital text in establishing precisely how it is that Christ functions as priest. As we shall see below, this view of Christ's exemplary priesthood flows from a particular one-sided reading of Hebrews 7. Jesus is seen as replacing – or at least surpassing – the old cultic priesthood of the temple by surpassing it in his death. Hebrews 7 is the earliest sustained witness to a long theological tradition of referring to Jesus as priest, even if our understanding of how it is Jesus is priest is remarkably underdeveloped in modern theological thought. Gerald O'Collins and Michael Keenan Jones note that, 'perhaps surprisingly, little reflection on Christ's own priesthood is available from modern works in Christology and soteriology'.[2] As O'Collins and Keenan Jones note, the theological foundation for Christ's priesthood is his role as mediator. Christ's humanity uniquely mediates our humanity with divinity. This mediation is a reflection of the understanding of the role of priest in the cultic sacrificial system of priesthood of Jesus' day. If we are to understand how Christ exercises his priestly ministry, we must look briefly at the role of the priest in the ancient world and in Judaism in particular.

Cultic priesthood

Priests were everywhere in the ancient world. Likewise, animal sacrifice was a regular feature of religious and daily life. It is worth noting that in scholarly terms it is perhaps harder to answer what priesthood is in the ancient world than we might expect.[3] Partly this is because our English word for 'priest' comes from a different word than is used in the Greek-speaking world for a religious 'official'. The English 'priest' derives from a contraction of the Greek *'presbuteros'* (from which we derive the term 'presbyter'). 'Presbyter' or elder is one of the favoured words for what we might call a Christian minister in the New Testament, as we shall see. The word for the kind of priest we are referring to when we speak of 'priesthood' in the ancient world is the Greek *'hiereus'* which derives from *'hieros'* and reflects the sacred or divine connotation of the ancient priesthood. It is used to translate the Hebrew for priest (*cohen*).[4]

Understandings of ancient priesthood have also been difficult to establish independently of the conceptual framework of notions of medieval Christian priesthood in scholarship following in the wake of the European Reformation. Medieval understandings of priesthood became the norm that Post-Reformation figures either rejected or modified in Reformed tradition or affirmed and modified in Catholic circles. Albert Henrichs cites Mary Beard and John North with approval when they note how difficult it is to separate our contemporary and Christian notions of ministerial priesthood when using the term 'priest' of an ancient figure. They argue that the 'decision to translate any given title by the word "priest" not only involves imposing our own categories, but also may obscure from us the distinctive nature of that official's role in his [sic] own society'.[5]

Sacrifice was an essential part of the role of the 'hiereus'. Priests offered animal life and gifts to various gods in a pagan context, while the Israelites differed in offering sacrifice to the God of Israel alone. Sacrifices could be and were offered by those who were not priests in the ancient world. There is evidence of this in the Hebrew Bible. The first sacrifice mentioned in the Bible is offered by Abel, with no indication that he is a priest (Genesis 4.4). Further, while animal sacrifice was an essential part of the role of the priest in the ancient world, the role of priesthood was likely wider than animal sacrifice alone. We see this in the Old Testament in, for example, the consultation of the priest concerning the uncleanliness or cleanliness of lepers (Leviticus 13—14). In the first century AD, Josephus (the Jewish historian who is one of our main sources for the Judaism of Jesus' day) ascribes a variety of functions to the Jewish priesthood beyond simply animal sacrifice as administrators of general affairs and conduct in public life.[6]

The act of animal sacrifice offered the life of the animal to God, for a variety of reasons from thanksgiving to appeasement for sin. The role of the priest in offering this animal sacrifice to God on behalf of others means that the priest is seen as a mediator figure. We see this mediatory role not only in Jewish priesthood – the priest offering sacrifices on behalf of the people, the high priest offering sacrifice for sin on the Day of Atonement – but also in wider Hellenistic society. Henrichs cites the example of Plato's definition of the spiritual as mediating between the earthly and heavenly and the role of priestly figures in 'interpreting and transporting human things to the gods and divine things to men; entreaties and sacrifices from below, and ordinances and requitals from above: being midway between, it makes each to supplement the other, so that the whole is combined in one'.[7] He notes further how such a mediatory role also leads to the priest becoming so closely associated with the divine that the priest can become a quasi-divine figure.

Gradually a system emerged in Israel by which only Aaron's descendants were permitted to offer sacrifices. In Exodus 28, the Lord tells Moses to consecrate Aaron and his sons to serve as priests, a statute which is made perpetual for 'him and for his descendants after him' in Exodus 28.43. In time, a second 'priestly' order evolved of Levites – descendants of Levi, not descended through Aaron – who, while not priests offering sacrifice, were permitted to assist those called to serve as priests within this sacrificial system (see Numbers 8.19, 22 and 18.1–7). The particular calling to priesthood of the sons of Aaron and the particular calling to serve as assistant and attendants of the sons of Levi is granted through biological descent. The seriousness with which this particular assigning of tasks in the worship of God is made clear to Aaron:

> So bring with you also your brothers of the tribe of Levi, your ancestral tribe, in order that they may be joined to you, and serve you while you and your sons with you are in front of the tent of the covenant. They shall perform duties for you and for the whole tent. But they must not approach either the utensils of the sanctuary or the altar, otherwise both they and you will die. (Numbers 18.2–3)

In addition to this particularity within the order of Levites as assistants and the cultic priesthood descended through Aaron, there was further particularity within the priesthood itself. For example, only the high priest was permitted to enter the Holy of Holies and then only on the day of Atonement (Leviticus 16).

Later Israelites differed from their pagan neighbours – at least theologically – not only in insisting on the Aaronic descent of their priests, but insisting that all sacrifice could only take place in the temple in Jerusalem. We see this reflected in the Samaritan woman's discussion with Jesus in John 4: 'Our ancestors worshipped on this mountain, but you say that the place where people must worship is in Jerusalem' (John 4.20). The use of the plural 'you' here along with the Samaritan woman's opening question in John 4.9 ('How is it that you, a Jew, ask a drink of me, a woman of Samaria?') suggest that the Samaritan woman is viewing Jesus as representative of Jewish attitudes towards right worship.

This restriction of sacrifice to Jerusalem is understood to have been enforced in the reforms to worship in Jerusalem enacted in the seventh century BC by Josiah (recounted in slightly different versions in 2 Kings 22—23 and in 2 Chronicles 34—35). Josiah rediscovers the book of the law (2 Kings 22.11; 2 Chronicles 34.14–16), proclaims it to the people (2 Kings 23.2, 2 Chronicles 34.30) and sets about reforming heterodox practice and pagan worship. A long tradition identifies Josiah's centralization of the temple cult with his rediscovery of the book of Deuteronomy, and especially Deuteronomy 12.13–14:

> Take care that you do not offer your burnt-offerings at any place you happen to see. But only at the place that the LORD will choose in one of your tribes – there you shall offer your burnt-offerings and there you shall do everything I command you.

In the first century AD, Josephus writes of the suitability of having only one place in which sacrifice is permitted and God worshipped: 'There ought also to be but one temple for one God; for likeness is the constant foundation of agreement. This temple ought to be common to all, because he is the common God of all.'[8]

There is some evidence that while Josephus might be reflecting the majority view within Judaism of the first century, there are also some other sites outside of Judea in which cultic priests offered sacrifices to the God of Israel. Josephus himself writes of a Jewish temple in Egypt located at Leontopolis and archaeological evidence has emerged of another temple associated with a military garrison in Egypt at Elephantine.[9] Moreover, Jordan Rosenblum has surveyed evidence of the extent of the practice of animal sacrifice at home altars to suggest that there is limited but unexpected evidence of the practice of animal sacrifice at home altars outside of the cultic priesthood required by the Jewish Law. However, he notes that it is not perhaps unexpected as a widespread feature of ancient Mediterranean society in which Jews lived and of which they were a part.[10] While Jesus' prediction in John 4.21 that the time is coming when worship will no longer take place in Jerusalem, this evidence for priestly sacrifice outside of Jerusalem in Jesus' day remains out of step with the normative view. The theological focus we find on the Jerusalem temple was reflected in the size of annual pilgrimage to Jerusalem. The corresponding wealth of the Jerusalem temple (which would be the cause of its sacking and desolation under Antiochus Epiphanes in the second century BC and contribute to its destruction by the Romans in AD 70) demonstrate the importance of the Jerusalem temple as the focus of worship and site of the sacrifice performed by the priesthood descended through Aaron.

We have described this cultic background briefly because it helps us to understand a little more clearly how it is Jesus functions as priest within Hebrews 7. It also helps us to see how from the point of view of cultic priesthood from both the Jewish and pagan priesthoods of Jesus' day, Jesus' priesthood seems particularly unlikely. As we shall see, the unlikeliness is not so much on where worship is to be focused and sacrifice made, but on who it is performing the sacrifice and what or who is the object of sacrifice. It will be this unlikeliness in terms of the cultic conventions of Jesus' day which will be our focus and is a particular aid in overcoming the clericalism which is the focus of our argument.

Jesus as priest

Jesus' priesthood is unlikely and not at all obvious within the cultic conventions of the day. He is not from the right family. We see him offer no animal sacrifice in a priestly role. This foundation will be essential to how we conceive of the ordained priesthood as grounded in Christ's priesthood, and liberative of the calling of each and every person of God.

The essential text in the New Testament for establishing the nature of Christ's priesthood is the letter to the Hebrews. Here we see set out a robust doctrine of how Christ is priest and what this means for the Christian life, and what it is that Christ's priesthood has achieved. Some argue that this makes Hebrews unique among the New Testament canon and that no other biblical author considers Christ to be priest. Reasons for this include Hebrews' fairly late date of composition – after the destruction of the Jerusalem temple and the end of the role of the Jewish high priest – which sees Hebrews as a piece of sustained theological reflection both on the death of Christ and on the events that had taken place in Jerusalem in the year 70.

More recently, Nicholas Perrin has convincingly demonstrated that the presentation of Jesus as priest and the application of priestly themes to Christ is more widespread throughout the New Testament as a whole.[11] The evidence he collects suggests allusions to Jesus adopting and transcending roles and actions reserved for the cultic priesthood of Jesus' day. For example, he points to the cleansing of the leper in Mark 1.40–45 in which Jesus seems immune to the potential for cultic impurity as a result of the contact with the leper and further:

> Jesus' instructions after the cleansing ('See that you say nothing to anyone, but go, show yourself to the priest and offer for your cleansing what Moses commanded, for a proof to them' [Mark 1.44]) are equally telling. Ordinarily, the leper would have had to consult the priest prior to his having been declared clean (Leviticus 13—14). That Jesus essentially skips this step, however, implies that he has taken this priestly judgment on himself.[12]

The argument for the presentation of Jesus as priest is perhaps strongest in the Gospel according to St John. In fact, some argue that Jesus is presented by John not only as priest but high priest, echoing the theological reflection on Christ's priesthood we shall encounter in Hebrews below. John Paul Heil argues that the 'Johannine Jesus does function as high priest, not in the systematic and sweeping manner of the Letter to the Hebrews, but in a more subtle and symbolic way.'[13] He points especially to the seamless robe of John 19.23 as a deliberate allusion to the high priestly garment which is described by the first-century Jewish historian Josephus as similarly seamless, 'not composed of two pieces, nor was it sewed together upon the shoulders and the sides, but it was one long vestment'.[14] The soldiers' decision not to tear the robe (John 19.24) like-wise echoes the high-priestly robe which was woven so as not to be torn (Exodus 28.32). The high-priestly garment itself represented the unity of the people of Israel. In this light, John's description of Jesus' seamless robe here both unexpectedly casts Jesus in the role of high priest but also, as Heil notes, through the robe's not being torn 'the irony of Gentiles pre-serving the seamless tunic of the high priest Jesus indicates Jesus' self-sacrifice death unifies all believers into a universal people composed of Jews and Gentiles'.[15]

What is important for our purposes here is to note that Jesus' potential role as high priest is an unexpected one, which is as much in continuity with cultic notions as it transforms them in unexpected ways: 'it is new and different, as Jesus sacrifices himself rather than an animal; and it is unique, since Jesus is the one and only true high priest in contrast to a plurality of Jewish high priests'.[16] Moreover, Jesus' high priestly task is one that consecrates others to share in this priestly task to unite the children of God.

Perrin agrees with Heil that Jesus is presented as a priestly figure, and as high priest in particular.[17] Two episodes to which Perrin draws attention are important for seeing how Christ functions as priest. First, he points to the anointing of Jesus by Mary at Bethany (John 12.1–8), suggesting that this anointing is 'a kind of high priestly anointing, akin the oil anointing that the high priests would undergo ... Jesus must undergo such an oil anointing because he is about to enter the atoning space of the unseen temple – through his death'.[18] Seen in this light, he argues, the subsequent washing of the disciples' feet by Jesus in John 13 takes on a new resonance. Not simply a sign of Jesus' humility, the washing of his disciples' feet as a parallel to the ritual cleansing required by priests before entering sacred space becomes a means by which 'Jesus now extends the priestly prerogative to the disciples'.[19] This implied 'consecration' of his disciples in itself implies a kind of priestly act. This insight of the priestly associations of the act of foot-washing will become an important insight on which to reflect below in Chapter 6 as we consider the priestliness of the order of deacons, as the foot-washing in John 13 is regularly associated with the ministry of the diaconate.

Part of the difficulty in establishing a clear understanding of how Jesus functions as priest outside of the letter to the Hebrews is the allusive and sometimes overlapping nature of the imagery used. For example, John's presentation of Jesus as God's new tabernacle – 'the Word became flesh and lived [or 'tabernacled'] among us' (John 1.14) is as much presenting Jesus as the new temple as in a priestly mediator role. The close connection of these motifs obvious and therefore any straightforward reading of Jesus as priest is not always easy. John 1.51 offers perhaps the best example of this. The promise to Nathaniel that he 'will see heaven opened and the angels of God ascending and descending upon the Son of Man' (John 1.51) alludes to Jacob's ladder (Genesis 28.12). The allusion within the biblical text seems to focus on the site as mediating God's presence: 'How awesome is this place! This is none other than the house of God, and this is the gate of heaven' (Genesis 28.17). Jacob's response – to establish an altar – confirms this (Genesis 28.18). However, this imagery is complicated by evidence of Jewish interpretation of this passage that sees Jacob himself as the mediator figure and which therefore establishes an even closer connection between priestly and temple imagery. Christopher Rowland has argued convincingly that it is the personal mediatory role to which John is alluding in this passage.[20]

Likewise, images of Jesus as the restorer of the temple may look toward kingly images as much as priestly ones – especially as these roles did not always overlap. Again Perrin notes: 'While the association between the Johannine Jesus and the eschatological temple does not prove that John also regarded Jesus as a (high) priest, it does make render such a construal plausible, not least on account of the close conceptual connection between sacred space and priests in Jewish antiquity.'[21]

Perhaps the clearest priestly act in the New Testament is the celebration of the Last Supper. Here we see Jesus' death is cast in sacrificial terms. From the earliest days of theological reflection on the necessity of Jesus' death we see that death cast as a sacrifice: 'For our paschal lamb, Christ, has been sacrificed' (1 Corinthians 5.7). In the Gospel of John, from which the institution of the Eucharist in the Last Supper is notable by its absence, Jesus' death occurs at the time the lambs were being slaughtered (John 19.14), which may identify him with the sacrificial lamb.[22] The language Jesus uses in the Last Supper makes his death the subject of sacrifice reflected in 1 Corinthians 11.23–25:

> For I received from the Lord what I also handed on to you, that the Lord Jesus on the night when he was betrayed took a loaf of bread, and when he had given thanks, he broke it and said, 'This is my body that is for you. Do this in remembrance of me.' In the same way he took the cup also, after supper, saying, 'This cup is the new covenant in my blood. Do this, as often as you drink it, in remembrance of me.'

The parallel texts to this passage (Mark 14.22–24, Matthew 26.26–29 and Luke 22.19–20) also underline that Christ's death is sacrificial. Blood sacrifices were especially associated with the forging of new covenants between God and God's people. For example, God's covenant with Noah (Genesis 9.9) is preceded by Noah's animal sacrifice (Genesis 8.20) and it is the sacrifice that prompts God to make good on his promise of a covenant.[23] The language of 'new covenant' associated with the shedding of Christ's blood is therefore significant.

However, this equation of the death of Christ with a sacrifice that establishes a new covenant does not necessarily mean that Christ is exercising a priestly role. It is the fact that Jesus equates his impending death with a sacrifice which establishes a new covenant that renders this act priestly. Christ is both sacrificial victim and priest here. Christ is both offered as sacrifice and the one who is offered in sacrifice. This too means that his priesthood is unlikely and expected – the sacrificial victim and sacrificing priest are one and the same.

The irony here is that those who would put him to death think they are the ones who are taking life from him. Christ's priestly act in the Last Supper defies those who would extinguish him of succeeding their aim. Their attempt at extinguishing his life, through Christ's priestly and sacrificial act, will become the means by which he restores life and defeats death. Rowan Williams writes powerfully of how Christ's priestly action nullifies his executioners attempts to extinguish life:

> By resigning himself into the signs of food and drink, putting himself into the hands of other agents, he signifies his forthcoming helplessness and death. He announces his death by 'signing' himself as a thing, to be handled and consumed ... God's act in Jesus forestalls the betrayal, provides in advance for it: Jesus binds himself to vulnerability before he is bound (literally) by human violence. Thus, those who are at table with him, who include those who will betray, desert and repudiate him, are, if you like, frustrated as betrayers, their job is done for them by their victim. By his surrender 'into' the passive forms of food and drink he makes void and powerless the impending betrayal, and more, makes his betrayers his guests and debtors, making with them the promise of divine fidelity, the covenant, that cannot be negated by their unfaithfulness.[24]

We have spent some time reflecting on how Christ is presented as priestly or as priest in the New Testament outside Hebrews as it is important to see reflected more widely the themes that the author of the letter to the Hebrews sets out.

This brief survey underlies that the priesthood of Christ is a more widespread notion in earliest Christian thought than we might think, given the general lack of developed theological reasoning on precisely how it is Christ functions as priest. Perrin suggests that one of the reasons for overlooking the breadth of reflection on the priesthood of Christ in the New Testament has been a post-Reformation squeamishness on the part of some to rehabilitate any concept of cultic priesthood.[25] He argues strongly that a rediscovery of Jesus' priesthood is a vital theological task:

> If nothing else, such findings call for a little disciplinary self-reflection. NT studies has relegated Jesus' priesthood to the cellblock of theological obscurities for far too long – and this error needs atoning. It is high time we declare Jesus the priest's release and make right our debts for any theological distortions incurred. Just what distortions these might be is a separate but nonetheless crucial question.[26]

Our consideration of Christ's priesthood as an unlikely candidate for priesthood and yet showing us a priesthood that is foundational for ordained ministry is a small step towards redressing these theological distortions. In John's Gospel we begin to get hints of what the consequence of this unlikely priesthood are for the unity of humankind that Christ's death will have achieved. We have also already begun to see that while Christ's priesthood is unexpected it is both in continuity with, and a challenge to, cultic notions of priesthood of his day. We shall see how in the letter to the Hebrews the author wrestles with the cultic conventions of priesthood to in an attempt to demonstrate precisely how Jesus' priesthood is simultaneously in continuity with the cultic priesthood (to establish that Jesus is in fact priest) and yet distinct from and transcends it (to establish the superior efficacy of Christ's priesthood). We will argue that this offers us an important theological foundation for ministry which overcomes the potential for clericalist patterns of ministry in all parts of the Church.

Jesus' priesthood according to Hebrews

The concept of Christ's priesthood is so central to the theology of the letter to the Hebrews that it's not possible for us to expound it in any great depth here.[27] Instead we shall survey how this theology of priesthood helps us to build a theology of ministry that overcomes the potential for clericalism in the Church. Central to this will be understanding how the author of the letter to the Hebrews reflects on the nature of Christ's priesthood to explain a potential criticism for Christ's role as priest which would cut off any claim that Christ has to be considered priest at the pass. Namely, the fact that Christ is unable to exercise *any* priesthood because he is not of priestly lineage and descent.

The genealogies of Matthew and Luke differ. Matthew's emphasizes Jesus' claim to kingship of the Jewish people through David. For Matthew, Jesus is emphatically 'the son of David, the son of Abraham' (Matthew 1.1). For Luke, Jesus is 'son of Adam, son of God' (Luke 3.37). For neither does Jesus' earthly ancestry render him able to serve the cultic priesthood as a son of Levi. Jesus' priestly ministry is decidedly unlikely from the view of the requirements of Aaronic or even Levitical descent.

The author of the epistles to the Hebrews addresses this challenge. How can Jesus be priest when he is not a suitable candidate for earthly priesthood?

The groundwork for Jesus' priesthood is laid in Hebrews 2. Rather than beginning with a particular lineage, Jesus' humanity is the foundation: 'Since, therefore, the children share flesh and blood, he himself likewise shared the same things' (Hebrews 2.14). Jesus becomes flesh to share in our flesh in order to destroy death. The humanity that is common to us all thus becomes the foundational principle of Jesus' claim to priesthood: 'he had to become like his brothers and sisters in every respect, so that he might be a merciful and faithful high priest in the service of God, to make a sacrifice of atonement for the sins of the people' (Hebrews 2.17). It is worth noting here the continuity and discontinuity with the cultic priesthood. Jesus does not share *in* the Levitical priesthood through descent from Aaron, but instead shares *with* the Levitical priesthood that which he shares with the entirety of humanity. However, the need for a sacrifice of atonement is not done away with (even though this too we shall see is transformed in Christ's priesthood from the repeated offering of cultic sacrifice).

The author's second step in establishing the ground for Jesus' priesthood is a contrast between Moses and Jesus. This is significant as it is through the revelation to Moses that the Levitical priesthood is established and it is Moses who consecrates Aaron priest (Leviticus 8). At Hebrews 3.1, Jesus is described as 'apostle and high priest'. The use of 'apostle' here is no mistake as it emphasizes that Jesus has been sent to function in this high priestly role. Initially, Moses' and Jesus' ministries are seen as comparable as both are faithful to their commission (Hebrews 3.2–3). Christ is subsequently presented as superior to Moses. This could perhaps already be inferred by the direct appointment of Christ as priest by God, in contrast to Moses being the vehicle of Aaron's appointment as priest. However, the author makes this explicit by contrasting Moses' faithfulness *in* God's house as *servant* (Hebrews 3.5) to Christ's faithfulness *over* God's house as a son (Hebrews 3.6).

Hebrews 5 continues the argument, with what could be a mission statement for the Jewish priesthood of Jesus' day:

> Every high priest chosen from among mortals is put in charge of things pertaining to God on their behalf, to offer gifts and sacrifices for sins. He is able to deal gently with the ignorant and wayward, since he himself is subject to weakness; and because of this he must offer sacrifice for his own sins as well as for those of the people. And one does not presume to take this honour, but takes it only when called by God, just as Aaron was. (Hebrews 5.1–4)

The author finds similarity between Jesus' priesthood and that of Aaron in that both are called by God. Christ's appointment as priest is – however – contrasted with that of Aaron. Christ as Son is begotten by God (Hebrews 5.5). The author of Hebrews goes on to prefigure the argument developed in greater detail in Hebrews 7 by drawing on Psalm 110.4: 'You are a priest for ever according to the order of Melchizedek.'

The text of Psalm 110 becomes vital for the argument of Hebrews here. It has already been applied to Christ twice by the author at Hebrews 1.3 and 1.13. In these passages, Jesus' sitting at the right hand of God draws on Psalm 110.1. This verse is repeated at Hebrews 5.5 to be bolstered by Psalm 110.4 at Hebrews 5.6. Psalm 110.4 becomes a key verse in understanding how the author of Hebrews develops their account of Jesus' priesthood as they find in this verse a solution to the unexpectedness of Jesus' priesthood from the point of view of the cultic priesthood, and also a signal that Jesus' priesthood transcends the cultic priesthood in which he is not qualified to serve. As we shall see in Hebrews 7, this verse provides the author with a model of priesthood that is eternal – 'a priest for ever' – unlike the transitory priesthood of earthly high priests.

The figure of Melchizedek is also key. He is the first priest mentioned in the biblical text (at Genesis 14.18) and is not a priest of the order of Aaron. The author of Hebrews traces Jesus' priesthood not through the order of Aaron but of Melchizedek (Hebrews 5.10). The phrase 'high priest according to the order of Melchizedek' becomes something of a refrain, repeated at Hebrews 7.10. We should note that this both points towards the unlikeliness of Jesus' priesthood from the point of view of the cultic system of Jesus' day, but also the continuity with patterns of priesthood found in the biblical text. The author of Hebrews finds another pattern of priestly ministry in the text other than those that had predominated in the cultic system of Jesus' day and underlines that both the transitory earthly priesthood of Aaron given through Moses and the eternal priesthood of Christ find their origins in a faithful response to God.

Hebrews 7 is the keystone of the argument for the nature of Christ's priesthood as it is unfolded by the author of the letter to the Hebrews. The figure of Melchizedek is once again key. At Genesis 14.18–20, Melchizedek appears without introduction, blesses Abram (Abraham) who gives him a tenth of everything, and exits stage right. The author of Hebrews develops this mysterious appearance in the biblical text: 'without father, without mother, without genealogy, having neither beginning of days nor end of life, but resembling the Son of God, he remains a priest for ever' (Hebrews 7.3). As Alan Mitchell notes,

> this description of Melchizedek's unusual pedigree favours a distinction between his priesthood and the Levitical priesthood, whose lineage was known. Hebrews presents Melchizedek as the type of a priesthood that is superior to the Levitical priesthood in order to establish a basis for the high priesthood of Christ.[28]

Hebrews 7.7 further makes use of the fact that Abraham pays tithes to Melchizedek (Genesis 14.20) to demonstrate the superiority of Christ's priesthood. As it is of the 'order of Melchizedek' and Melchizedek received tithes from Abraham, so Christ's priesthood is superior to the Levitical priesthood that descends from Abraham through Levi (Hebrews 7.9–10).

For our purposes, the central observation of the author of Hebrews concerns these unexpected origins for Christ's priesthood. This is spelt out clearly at Hebrews 7.13–16:

> Now the one of whom these things are spoken belonged to another tribe, from which no one has ever served at the altar. For it is evident that our Lord was descended from Judah, and in connection with that tribe Moses said nothing about priests. It is even more obvious when another priest arises, resembling Melchizedek, one who has become a priest, not through a legal requirement concerning physical descent, but through the power of an indestructible life.

The apparent problem of Jesus' descent from the tribe of Judah which seemingly rules him out of adopting a priestly role is turned into the foundation of an eternal priesthood. In fact, the unexpectedness of Christ's particular priesthood outside of Levitical descent is the means by which priestly mediation and immediacy of divine presence is available not only to those of a particular descent or tribe. Mitchell puts this best: 'Despite the fact that he descended from a tribe that never served at the altar, the advent of his priesthood brought about a broader means of access to God.'[29] This is not only because this priesthood is grounded in the humanity of Christ and not any particular lineage of descent as we saw above, but because of its eternity: he holds his priesthood permanently, because he continues for ever. Consequently he is able for all time to save those who approach God through him, since he always lives to make intercession for them (Hebrews 7.24–25). We can note that this particular unexpected calling has expanded the ability of all people to come into the presence of God through the mediation of Christ's particular and unexpected priesthood.

The remainder of the argument of the letter to the Hebrews builds on the discovery of this unexpected priesthood. It compares Christ's priesthood with the cultic priesthood of Jesus' day. Christ serves in the heavens (Hebrews 8.1), the Levitical priesthood serves in a replica of the heavens (Hebrews 8.5). Again the author notes that Christ would not be able to serve in this replica (Hebrews 8.4) even while he is in heaven. Christ enters heaven once and for all (Hebrews 9.12, 10.11), the high priest has to enter once a year (Hebrews 9.7, 25). Christ offers his own blood as both priest and victim (Hebrews 9.12). This reflection echoes the priestly elements of the Last Supper narratives we traced above. Christ's blood offering removes sin for all time (Hebrews 9.26–28), while the blood sacrifice of animals must be offered again and again (Hebrews 9.25).

The shameful history of Christian antisemitism means that it is important to read these comparisons carefully to avoid making a supercessionistic misreading of the text the basis of our theological foundation for Christ's priesthood as a model of the exercise of ordained ministry and priesthood. There are some places in the text of Hebrews where the author indicates that the new covenant abrogates the old: 'in speaking of "a new covenant", he has made the first one obsolete'. However, to read the entirety of Hebrews through the lens of this passage is to misread the letter. We have already noted the care with which the author of Hebrews points to the faithfulness of Moses (Hebrews 3.2–5). Indeed, the author neither departs entirely from the biblical witness nor dismisses the logic of the priestly system altogether. In basing the priesthood of Christ on the order of Melchizedek he reads the existing biblical witness in a new way in the light of the death and resurrection of Christ. Likewise, the theological reflection on Christ's death as resurrection in which Christ is seen both as victim and priest does not entirely abrogate the underlying conceptual framework of the biblical witness from which the cultic priesthood arose, even as it reconfigures this witness towards Christ.

This is also an important observation for us as we conclude this chapter on how it is Christ functions as priest. We have seen how throughout the New Testament priestly and high priestly categories are applied to Christ, even though he is not eligible to serve the earthly priesthood. Christ's priesthood is different from the priesthood of his day. He offers no animal sacrifice, even while we can see him taking on other priestly roles. Christ's priesthood is unexpected. In Hebrews, its basis is in our shared humanity. Christ's priesthood is expansive. It expands the concept of priesthood beyond received categories. The foot-washing in John's Gospel may indicate a widening of his priesthood to those to which he confers a share in this ministry regardless of their lineage or descent. Christ's priesthood, signified in the seamless robe, is unifying – intended to unite Jew and Gentile and all humanity to God.

However, while Christ's priesthood is in important ways distinct from the priesthood of Jesus' day, it is important to note that in order to appreciate how it is Jesus functions as priest there is also a conceptual continuity. Christ's priesthood is established in an earthly sacrifice yet differs in that he sacrifices himself. Christ's priesthood is exercised through sacrifice, but it is Christ who lays down his life as both victim and priest. At the Last Supper where Christ's priestly ministry is most apparent, this act of sacrifice takes place in the context of the faithful celebration of Passover and the daily Jewish tradition of prayers over meals. Christ transforms these so that these celebrations become the site of the new life and these new ritual acts become a means to point more clearly to him, and so that we may call to mind what he is about to do for each of us and for our salvation. Here we see the seeds of ministry that is robust in its defence against clericalism: unexpected, expansive, unifying, faithful and, most importantly, ever centred on Christ and Christ's unexpected, expansive, unifying, faithful priestly witness.

Most importantly, Christ frustrates the expectations of who might be called to serve as priest and expands our vision of what priesthood might be. This will be an essential feature of our understanding of how to exercise ordained ministry in a way that is decidedly anti-clericalist and, like's Christ priestly ministry, liberates the capacity and enables fullness of life for all those whom we are called to serve.

Notes

1 Rowan Williams, 'Women and the Ministry: A Case for Theological Seriousness' in Monica Furlong (ed.), *Feminine in the Church* (London: SPCK, 1984), pp. 11–24 (p. 15).

2 Gerald O'Collins and Michael Keenan Jones, *Jesus Our Priest: A Christian Approach to the Priesthood of Christ* (Oxford: Oxford University Press, 2010).

3 See, for example, Albert Henrichs, 'What is a Greek Priest?' in Beate Dignas and Kai Trampedach (eds), *Practitioners of the Divine: Greek Priests and Religious Figures from Homer to Heliodorus* (Washington, DC: Center for Hellenic Studies, 2008), available at: https://chs. harvard.edu/chapter/introduction-what-is-a-greek-priest-albert-henrichs/ [accessed 28.06.2021].

4 On the relation between these terms and the later development of Christian ministry, see, for example, Thomas O'Loughlin, 'Ministries' in Juliette Day and Benjamin Gordon-Taylor, *The Study of Liturgy and Worship: An Alcuin Guide* (London: SPCK, 2013), pp. 82–90.

5 Mary Beard and John North, *Pagan Priests: Religion and Power in the Ancient World* (London: Duckworth, 1990), p. 3 cited in Henrichs, 'Greek Priest', Appendix #20.

6 Josephus, *Against Apion* 2.184, available at: www.perseus.tufts. edu/hopper/text?doc=Perseus%3Atext%3A1999.01.0216%3Abook %3D2%3Asection%3D184 [accessed 8.09.2021].

7 Plato, Symposium, 202e, available at: www.perseus.tufts. edu/hopper/text?doc=Perseus%3Atext%3A1999.01.0174%3Atext %3DSym.%3Asection%3D202e [accessed 8.09.2021].

8 Josephus, *Against Apion* 2.184, available at: www.perseus.tufts. edu/hopper/text?doc=Perseus%3Atext%3A1999.01.0216%3Abook %3D2%3Asection%3D184 [accessed 8.09.2021].

9 Josephus, *Jewish War* 7.10.4, available at: http://penelope.uchicago. edu/josephus/war-7.html [accessed 8.09.2021]. See, for example, Stephen G. Rosenberg, 'The Jewish Temple at Elephantine', *Near Eastern Archaeology* 67.1 (March 2004), pp. 4–13.

10 Jordan Rosenblum, 'Home is Where the Hearth Is: A Consideration of Jewish Household Sacrifice in Antiquity' in Caroline Johnson Hodge et al. (eds), *'The One Who Sows Bountifully': Essays in Honor of Stanley K. Stowers* (Providence, RI: Brown Judaic Studies, 2013), pp. 153–63.

11 See Nicholas Perrin, *Jesus the Priest* (Grand Rapids, MI: Baker Academic, 2018) and 'Jesus as Priest in the Gospels', *The Southern Baptist Journal of Theology* 22.2 (2018), pp. 81–99.

12 Perrin, 'Jesus as Priest', p. 84.

13 John Paul Heil, 'Jesus as the Unique High Priest in the Gospel of John', *The Catholic Biblical Quarterly* 57.4 (October 1995), pp. 729–45, 730.

14 Josephus, *Antiquities* 3.161, available at: www.perseus.tufts.edu/ hopper/text?doc=Perseus%3Atext%3A1999.01.0146%3Abook%3D3 %3Asection%3D159 [accessed 9.09.2021].

15 Heil, 'Unique High Priest', p. 745.

16 Heil, 'Unique High Priest', p. 730.

17 See also O'Collins and Keenan Jones, *Jesus Our Priest*, pp. 24–6.

18 Perrin, 'Jesus as Priest', p. 91.

19 Perrin, 'Jesus as Priest', p. 91.

20 Christopher Rowland, 'John 1.51, Jewish Apocalyptic and Targumic Tradition', *New Testament Studies* 30.4 (1984), pp. 498–504. This chapter is dedicated to him. The description of Christ in similarly personal mediatory terms is found elsewhere in the New Testament. 1 Timothy 2.5 casts Jesus as the sole mediatory figure, echoing language of priestly mediation we will find in Hebrews.

21 Perrin, 'Jesus as Priest', p. 87.

22 See Raymond Brown, *The Death of the Messiah: Volume One* (London: Doubleday, 1998), p. 847. Early in John's Gospel, Jesus is described as the 'lamb of God' suggesting Jesus as the object of sacrifice (John 1.29, 36).

23 Genesis 8.21; cf. Genesis 6.18.

24 Rowan Williams, 'Sacraments of the New Society' in Rowan Williams, *On Christian Theology* (Oxford: Blackwell, 2000), pp. 209–21, 215–16.

25 For the diametrically opposed view, see Robin Ward, *On Christian Priesthood* (London: Continuum, 2011).

26 Perrin, 'Jesus as Priest', pp. 97–8.

27 See, for example, O'Collins and Keenan Jones, *Jesus Our Priest*, pp. 45–67; R. B. Jamieson, *Jesus' Death and Heavenly Offering in Hebrews* (Cambridge: Cambridge University Press, 2019); Nicholas Moore, 'Sacrifice, Session, and Intercession: The End of Christ's Offering in Hebrews', *Journal for the Study of the New Testament* 42.4 (May 2020), pp. 521–41; David M. Moffitt, 'It is Not Finished: Jesus' Perpetual Atoning Work as the Heavenly High Priest in Hebrews' in J. C. Laansma, G. H. Guthrie and C. L. Westfall (eds), *So Great a Salvation: A Dialogue on the Atonement in Hebrews* (Bloomsbury: T&T Clark, 2019), pp. 157–75 and 'Jesus as Interceding High Priest and Sacrifice in Hebrews: A Response to Nicholas Moore', *Journal for the Study of the New Testament* 42.4 (May 2020), pp. 542–52.

28 Alan C. Mitchell, *Hebrews* (Collegeville, MN: Liturgical Press, 2007), p. 141.

29 Mitchell, *Hebrews*, p. 151.

2

Clericalism and the Priesthood of All Believers

Now there are varieties of gifts, but the same Spirit; and there are varieties of services, but the same Lord; and there are varieties of activities, but it is the same God who activates all of them in everyone. To each is given the manifestation of the Spirit for the common good. To one is given through the Spirit the utterance of wisdom, and to another the utterance of knowledge according to the same Spirit, to another faith by the same Spirit, to another gifts of healing by the one Spirit, to another the working of miracles, to another prophecy, to another the discernment of spirits, to another various kinds of tongues, to another the interpretation of tongues. All these are activated by one and the same Spirit, who allots to each one individually just as the Spirit chooses. (1 Corinthians 12.4–11)

In this chapter we consider the notion of the 'priesthood of all believers'. Like Christ's priesthood, the 'priesthood of all believers' is a phrase perhaps more often repeated in Christian circles as a commonplace than it is reflected upon. Rarely do those who use the phrase reflect as to how precisely a universal priesthood contributes to the flourishing or otherwise of the Christian life and each person's particular vocation.

Just as we saw that Christ's priesthood has been neglected as a subject of theological reflection, so too the 'priesthood of all believers'. Craig Nessan highlights this neglect: 'Instead of developing the fulsome potential of Luther's theology of vocation in tandem with justification, the universal priesthood of all believers lived out in the arenas of their daily lives has remained on the margins.'[1]

Hank Voss notes that one reason for this is that:

the vast scope of Luther's writings has contributed to a wide variety of opinions about his 'priesthood of all believers'. The only consensus is that it has repeatedly been misunderstood. Part of the problem is that Luther never wrote a systematic summary of his theology, so his thinking must be compiled from occasional pieces and then traced through stages of development.[2]

However, there are other reasons for the neglect of 'the priesthood of all believers' which are perhaps the polar opposite of the reasons for the neglect of what it means for Christ to be priest. While the priesthood of Christ may have been avoided as a subject of critical reflection through a Protestant squeamishness at the notion of priests, or a corresponding Catholic suspicion that too great a focus on the unique priesthood of Christ will undermine the Christian priesthood, the reluctance to reflect on the 'priesthood of all believers' may stem from ecumenical embarrassment. Tom Greggs makes this observation: 'attempted mutual recognition of orders has determined a degree of care exercised in relation to discussing this (reputedly) most Protestant of doctrines, which ostensibly seems to call into question the very nature of orders itself; best to suspend such discussions for the sake of unity, seems to be the collective wisdom'.[3]

In this chapter we will explore the concept of the priesthood of all believers and argue that far from freeing the Church from the potential for clericalism, it in fact runs the risk of clericalizing the entire Church rather than liberating every member of the Church to fulfil their particular vocation. We will argue that the relative lack of theological reflection on Christ's priesthood, mirrored in the relative lack of theological reflection on what it means to affirm the priesthood of all believers, is related to the potential for the priesthood of all believers to further rather than overcome the problem of clericalism within the Church. This runs against the very intention with which Martin Luther first introduced the concept of the 'priesthood of all believers' into the doctrinal phraseology of Christian thought.

We shall see he does so as an attempted solution to the clericalism of the ministerial priesthood he had experienced and was protesting against. We shall argue that the solution to clericalism is not to abolish ministerial priesthood – which even Luther does not suggest – but rather that the tendency to draw lines from the cultic priesthood to ministerial priesthood leaves the exercise of that priesthood open to the potential for clericalism. A ministerial priesthood that is exercised in such a way as to contribute towards the limitation of clericalism from church life needs, ironically, to focus rather more on the concept of priesthood. However, this concept of ministerial priesthood is not a reversion to the cultic priesthood, but rather requires a closer attention to the priesthood of Christ we explored above. The under-exploration of Christ's priesthood in the Church itself enables clericalism because it limits this constant return to Christ's priesthood as the source of all ministry and priesthood.

A kingdom of priests

The early Church seems to have foreseen the difficulty in establishing a Christian concept of ministerial priesthood on Christ's priesthood, without the corresponding danger of conflation notions of Christian and cultic priesthood. While it is true to say the language of 'priest' (*hiereus*) we traced above is only used individually of Christ in the New Testament, we see an evolution in Christian language that permits the use of the term to be applied to an individual over the course of the first two to three centuries AD.

This evolution begins early as we shall see in the first epistle of Clement to the Corinthians written around AD 96. Over those initial centuries the term 'priest' (*hiereus*) is initially reserved for Christ, then applied to the ministry of the bishop (*episcopos* or 'overseer') which is a term found in the New Testament.[4] Finally, it is applied to the ministry of elders or presbyters who share in the priestly ministry of the bishop. The use of all these terms derives only secondarily from any comparison to the cultic priesthood. It is the sharing in the priesthood of Christ that gives each their primary sense.

Before we look at this evolution in the use of the term 'priest' for Christian ministers, it's first important to look at the use of the term 'priest' in a Christian sense applied more widely than to just the ministry of Christ. At one level, this usage will point us towards Luther's understanding of the 'priesthood of all believers'. However, we shall see that the use of this 'priestly' language is also in some important ways distinct.

Paul describes his mission to the Gentiles in 'priestly' terms: 'a minister of Christ Jesus to the Gentiles in the priestly service of the gospel of God, so that the offering of the Gentiles may be acceptable, sanctified by the Holy Spirit' (Romans 15.16). It's likely that Paul uses this priestly language metaphorically (as the 'offering' of the Gentiles seems certain to be metaphorical) rather than a widening of the concept of priesthood to Christian ministry more generally.

Elsewhere, Paul applies the language of 'living sacrifice' to the Christian life (Romans 12.1). This recalls the language of cultic sacrifice. Rather than making a cultic offering, the Christian is called to offer the conduct of their lives. There is a priestly element of this that parallels Christ's priesthood. The Christian is both the one offering this living sacrifice and the living sacrifice that is offered. For our purposes it's important to note the verses that immediately follow. The shape of this living sacrifice 'differs according to the grace given to us' (Romans 12.6). In words that may stand as an anthem against clericalism, Paul exhorts his readers 'not to think of yourself more highly than you ought to think' (Romans 12.3) but to exercise the particular ministry to which they have been called.

The two major uses of the motif of priesthood in the New Testament for those other than Christ pre-empt the concept of the 'priesthood of all believers'. These are found in 1 Peter and the book of Revelation. In 1 Peter, the imagery of priesthood is used for the Church as a whole, which is called 'to be a holy priesthood, to offer spiritual sacrifices acceptable to God through Jesus Christ' (1 Peter 2.5). The application of the motif of priesthood to the whole community echoes the language of Exodus 19.6 which describes the people of Israel as 'a priestly kingdom and a holy nation'. We can see this more clearly in 1 Peter 2.9: 'you are a chosen race, a royal priesthood, a holy nation, God's own people'.

Donald Senior notes:

> some consider these texts the basis for a 'priesthood of believers' that, in effect, would deny the possibility of a specific priestly ministry in the church. But in referring to a 'priesthood' exercised by all Christians 1 Peter is neither affirming nor denying the possibility of a specific liturgical role in the church, just as the author of Exodus 19 could speak of the entire Israelite community as 'priestly' without thereby passing judgement on the Levitical priesthood.[5]

To understand how the priesthood of the Church is understood in 1 Peter, it's important both to recognize the allusion to Exodus 19 here and also the allusions to Hosea that follow in 1 Peter 2.10: 'Once you were not a people, but now you are God's people; once you had not received mercy, but now you have received mercy.'[6] The priestliness is both a sign of God's special favour as a chosen race. It is also possible that the author of 1 Peter sees the motif of the priestliness of the people as a whole as a mediator of God's grace to the nations and applies this to the nascent Christian community. For our purposes, just as we saw how the seamless robe of John's Gospel echoes the new unity of Jew and Gentile in the Church, so 1 Peter is also reflecting this new community of Jew and Gentile that the Christian community creates. This priestly language both unites a new community and sets them apart for the sake of those they serve. This is an important corrective to simply reading the later concept of the 'priesthood of all believers' out of 1 Peter.

Likewise, priestly motifs in Revelation are applied not to Christ but the redeemed as a whole. The entirety of the Church, both on earth and those who have died bearing witness to Christ, are described as 'priests' (Revelation 1.6; 5.10; 20.6). While Christ himself is not described in priestly terms, this use of priestly language is closely associated with the death of Christ as enabling this Christian priesthood. Christ's death as sacrifice has created this community of priests, which is closely associated with this general priesthood both at Revelation 1.6 and 5.10. One crucial feature in understanding this general priesthood is its multi-ethnic make-up. Christ's death ransoms 'for God saints from every tribe and tongue and people and nation' (Revelation 5.9) from which they are made to be a 'kingdom and priests serving our God' (Revelation 5.10). There is a universal, or at least multi-national, aspect to this priestly calling.

Two points are important for us to notice as we continue our development of an anti-clericalist approach to Christian ministry generally and ordained ministry in particular. First, this priestly language is used in a particular way. It demonstrates the closeness of the Christian community to the death of Christ as foundational. It also emphasizes that this community finds a new unity through this priestly identity akin to the priestly identity of God's people Israel as a nation chosen out of other nations, and potentially *for* the sake of those other nations as a vicarious priestly offering. Second, the application of a priestly motif to the entire community is only one of a number of images and motifs used of the Christian community. Moreover, images of priestly service of the entire Church and more direct identification of the Church as 'priests' sit alongside passages that see this calling as lived out according to particular ministries.

The priesthood of all believers

It is the Lutheran conception of the 'priesthood of all believers' to which we now turn. As we shall see, this conception was born out of a rejection of the particularity of ministries that had evolved in the medieval Church and the manner in which they were controlled and exercised.[7] However, we shall see that even Luther's understanding of the 'priesthood of all believers' does away with the particularity of calling, or the concept of particular callings within the Church *per se*. To read the priesthood of all believers simply as a call to generic vocation can become a means by which clericalism can run rife, as the particular vocation to which God is calling this or that person can be subsumed within an expectation that vocation take only one form or approved shape – the same for all believers.

Greggs notes that 'the priesthood of all believers has an easy habit of becoming a discussion of the priesthood of each believer, individually and independently, in which each of us is considered our own priest'.[8] He warns that 'the relation of the doctrine of the priesthood of all believers to issues of ecclesial polity and governance continues in contemporary ecclesiological discussion to the detriment of the positive theological content that identifying the church as a priesthood might offer'.[9] Greggs is right to note that, like discussion of Christ's priesthood, the theological significance of the 'priesthood of all believers' is underdeveloped in contemporary thought.

However, we will find that Greggs's location of the priesthood solely in the Church (without reference to the particular ministry of the ordained as a means of serving that priesthood) also runs the risk of promoting the very clericalism that refusing to identify priesthood with a particular '*clerus*' or group of people exercising that priesthood (which Greggs is keen to avoid). Guido de Graaff agrees that 'the import of that concept is easily overlooked, I would suggest, when it is used merely as an argument for increased lay (licensed) ministry'.[10] In fact, Greggs notes that Luther's conception of the '*priesthood* of all believers' denies any concept of laity.[11] This denial risks an homogenization of Christian witness which is both unbiblical and runs the risk of making the patterns of clericalism and creation of new forms of elite harder to diagnose.

Luther understands priesthood not to be bound up with a certain group of individuals in the life of the Church with corresponding power and status. His understanding has two elements. First, the equality of status of each Christian: 'there is really no difference between laymen and priests, princes and bishops, "spirituals" and "temporals," as they call them, except that of office and work, but not of "estate"; for they are all of the same estate'.[12]

Second, the role of baptism as the fundamental means of conferring that status on each Christian: 'through baptism all of us are consecrated to the priesthood ... whoever comes out the water of baptism can boast that he is already consecrated'.[13]

Greggs notes that Luther continues in 'the idea that priesthood passes to individuals; he just widens the number of individuals this involves'.[14] Having widened the circle of priesthood to include all the baptized, he then reverts to a different model of ministry that stops short of the homogenization of vocation on the grounds that this would be 'unseemly': 'just because we are all in like manner priests, no one must put himself forward and undertake, without our consent and election, to do what is in the power of all of us. For what is common to all, no one dare take upon himself without the will and the command of the community.'[15]

Indeed, one of the examples Luther gives to establish that all the baptized are priests presumes the very variety of vocations that the 'priesthood of all believers' potentially masks:

> If a little group of pious Christian laymen were taken captive and set down in a wilderness, and had among them no priest consecrated by a bishop, and if there in the wilderness they were to agree in choosing one of themselves, married or unmarried, and were to charge him with the office of baptizing, saying mass, absolving and preaching, such a man would be

as truly a priest as though all bishops and popes had consecrated him.[16]

There is an indissoluble element of polemic in Luther's understanding of the 'priesthood of all believers'. He is rejecting
the medieval exercise of priestly ministry and its associated
clericalist trapping and the misuse of power this entails 'issued
in such a pompous display of power, and such a terrible
tyranny ... through this perversion of things it has happened
that the knowledge of Christian grace, of faith, of liberty, and
altogether of Christ, has utterly perished, and has been suc-
ceeded by an intolerable bondage'.[17]

Greggs is right when he says that: 'rather than fundamentally
rethinking the issue, he [Luther] polemically responds to it'.[18]
There are, however, seeds of a positive doctrine of priesthood
from Luther's polemical rejection of the ministerial priesthood
of his day. Greggs tries to find these seeds by removing the
exercise of priesthood from individuals altogether and locating
the concept of priesthood within the Church as a whole:

The point of the priesthood of the church is not the so-called
priesthood of individuals in terms of their status or standing
in the leadership of the community; this is not the sort of priest
that Jesus was. It concerns, rather, the unity and singularity
of the church as a 'race' to use the Petrine language. Priesthood is a powerful way to express this, since one cannot be a
priest for oneself. A nation or race of priests is a nation which
is united through its inner structural ordering to God and to
other people. Priesthood requires not only relationality with
God but also relationality with other humans; in a nation of
priests, priesthood is the very form of sociality that creates
the community as a community which ministers God to each
other and each other to God. This radically undermines an
overemphasis on individualism.[19]

There is much to be commended in this vision. The view of the
Church as the locus of priesthood draws on the priestly nation

imagery of Exodus 19 and 1 Peter above. There are down-sides too that in focusing on the corporate priesthood of the Christian community the focus on the particular vocation of the individual Christian and the particular exercise of Christian freedom to which the individual is being called are overlooked. There are, however, other lines out of Luther's conception that do better than Greggs's 'priesthood of the church' in overcoming the potential for clericalism in the prioritizing of certain patterns of vocation or the potential abuse of power in dictating this or that vocation for an individual against the vocation to which that individual is ultimately being called.

A 'priesthood of the church' can all too easily become a 'priesthood of the majority'. One of the key vocations of the ordained ministry, we shall argue, is to consistently call the Church back to its common priesthood, and to recognize the common priesthood of each of its members. An essential part of this task is to recognize where clericalist elites are diminishing the capacity of others, majorities are excluding, and new forms of marginalization are taking hold. The fact of the ordained ministry exists as leaven to call the whole of the Church and especially the ordained to a greater share in priesthood after the manner of Christ.

Such a positive conception can be traced in Luther's understanding of the purpose of all ministry: 'ministers, servants, and stewards, who are to serve the rest in the ministry of the Word, for teaching the faith of Christ and the liberty of believers'.[20] Luther does recognize a distinction in how to nourish the priesthood of all believers, namely, that 'it is true that we are all equally priests, yet we cannot, nor, if we could, ought we all to minister and teach publicly'.[21]

This distinction demonstrates that there is a particularity that even Luther admits in ministries within the Church, albeit between those who should and should not teach and minister. This particularity is in keeping with the variety of vocation that we find on the pages of Scripture. We read in the letter to the Ephesians: 'the gifts he gave were that some would be apostles, some prophets, some evangelists, some pastors and

teachers, to equip the saints for the work of ministry, for building up the body of Christ' (Ephesians 4.11–12).

This variety of ministries exists to serve the entire body of
Christ 'to equip the saints' and 'build up the body of Christ'.
Luther's variety admits the category of those who should
and should not preach. He does not do away with the ministerial priesthood, but grounds that ministerial priesthood
on the common priesthood which all share through baptism.
Indeed, B. A. Gerrish notes that when the question arises 'of
how to check the growing band of eager, self-made preachers
who were overrunning Saxony ... Luther takes his stand on
the divinely-instituted system and the necessity for official cre-
dentials. The congregation becomes the laity, and over against
them stands the clergyman.'[22]

Luther is not eradicating the ministerial priesthood. He is
reforming it so that it finds its foundation not in a certain class
of persons, but in the baptized people of God as a whole. This
is an important insight. Part of this reformation is the means
by which ministerial priesthood is conferred or acknowledged.
It is not conferred by the elite but acknowledged by the entire
congregation: 'The preaching office is no more than a public
service which happens to be conferred upon someone by the
entire congregation, all the members of which are priests.'[23]
The means of discernment and conferral of orders is a necessary part of discerning who is called to take on this public
role. Luther emphasizes the congregational role as a means
of providing an 'objective' basis within the Church to overcome a potentially 'subjective' self-appointed elite. This insight
is an important means by which to overcome the potential
for clericalism in the selection and appointment of ordained
ministers.[24] However, it too is open to potential clericalist
abuse of power if the mechanisms of congregational discernment do not encourage privileging majority or particularly
favoured shapes of ministry. Do the processes by which clergy
callings are acknowledged and conferred truly belong to the
whole Church or do they represent a sphere of influence of a
clerical and self-replicating elite?

That some people are called to particular ministries in the body of life, and that some people are called to public 'priestly' ministry, we shall argue does not lead inevitably to clericalism. Indeed, this form of ordained ministry is one of the best antidotes to clericalism. Luther's stand for a particular public ministry against the self-appointed preachers is an example of how such ministry can serve to free the Church from clericalism as much as it has the potential to become clericalist itself. The call to ordained ministry is not a self-appointed one, but like all callings is allotted to the individual.

The 'priesthood of all believers' helps us identify some features of Christian ministry in general and ordained ministry in particular that it will be essential to carry over into our discussion of ministerial priesthood.

First, we see the New Testament could apply priestly language to the vocation of all Christians. Paul's use of the priestly language of 'living sacrifice' encourages us to see Christian life and ministry that requires us to devote the whole of our selves to the Christian life and priestly task.

Second, we see how in 1 Peter and Revelation how an essential feature of Christian priesthood is its transnational origin. Just as Christ's priesthood was no longer based on a particular line of descent, so the royal priesthood of the Church forms new community out of previous patterns of nationhood and delineation.

Third, we saw Luther's conception of the 'priesthood of all believers' was limited, as it risks homogenizing vocation and is potentially vulnerable to certain clericalist patterns, for example, prioritizing certain vocations over others or creating new self-appointed elites. It also risks clericalizing all vocation. However, we saw too that it contained some important insights to carry with us: the equality of status of all Christian vocation, the sharing in Christ's priesthood which is open to all Christians, the role of the entire Church in truly discerning and celebrating each particular vocation, and the role of particular ministries in serving that common priesthood. It is to those particular ministries we now turn.

Notes

1 Craig L. Nessan, 'Universal Priesthood of All Believers: Unfulfilled Promise of the Reformation', *Currents in Theology and Mission* 46.1 (January 2019), pp. 8–15 (p. 8).

2 Hank Voss, *The Priesthood of All Believers and the Missio Dei: A Canonical, Catholic, and Contextual Perspective* (Eugene, OR: Pickwick, 2016), Kindle Location 4723.

3 Tom Greggs, 'The Priesthood of No Believer: On the Priesthood of Christ and His Church', *International Journal of Systematic Theology* (17.4), pp. 374–98 (p. 376).

4 Acts 20.28; Philippians 1.1; 1 Timothy 3.2; Titus 1.7; cf. 1 Peter 2.25.

5 Donald Senior and Daniel Harrington, *1 Peter, Jude and 2 Peter* (Collegeville, MN: Liturgical Press, 2008), p. 61.

6 Hosea 2.23; cf. Hosea 1.6–7.

7 Greggs suggests that the 'reformers' ecclesial-political setting determines that they treat the priesthood of all believers dominantly as a negative doctrine about church order, so conditioned are they by the contextual settings in which they find themselves' (Greggs, 'Priesthood of No Believer', p. 374).

8 Greggs, 'Priesthood of No Believer', p. 377.

9 Greggs, 'Priesthood of No Believer', p. 377.

10 Guido de Graaff, 'Intercession as Political Ministry: Re-Interpreting the Priesthood of all Believers', *Modern Theology* 32.4 (2016), pp. 504–21.

11 Greggs, 'Priesthood of No Believer', p. 386.

12 Luther, Martin, *Open Letter to the Christian Nobility* (1520), p. 2, available at: https://web.stanford.edu/~jsabol/certainty/readings/Luther-ChristianNobility.pdf [accessed 31.10.2017]. See also Martin Luther, *On the Freedom of a Christian* (1520), p. 115, available at: https://sourcebooks.fordham.edu/mod/luther-freedomchristian.asp [accessed 13.12.2020]: 'Christ has obtained for us this favour, if we believe in Him, that, just as we are His brethren, and co-heirs and fellow kings with Him, so we should be also fellow priests with Him, and venture with confidence, through the spirit of faith, to come into the presence of God.'

13 Luther, *Open Letter*, p. 3.

14 Greggs, 'Priesthood of No Believer', p. 387.

15 Luther, *Open Letter*, p. 2. Luther repeats this idea in *On the Freedom of a Christian*, p. 117: 'For though it is true that we are all equally priests, yet we cannot, nor, if we could, ought we all to minister and teach publicly.'

16 Luther, *Open Letter*, p. 2.

17 Luther, *On the Freedom of a Christian*, p. 117.

18 Greggs, 'Priesthood of No Believer', p. 387.

19 Greggs, 'Priesthood of No Believer', p. 392.

20 Luther, *On the Freedom of a Christian*, pp. 116–17.

21 Luther, *On the Freedom of a Christian*, p. 117. See Voss, *Priesthood of All Believers*, Kindle Location 5007, for discussion of Luther's restriction of preaching, baptizing and celebrating the Eucharist to those who exercise a publicly acknowledged and conferred ministry. The universal priesthood of all believers means that all can perform these acts, but only *in extremis*. Luther is clear that the exception does not prove the rule.

22 B. A. Gerrish, 'Priesthood and Ministry in the Theology of Luther', *Church History* 34.4 (December 1965), pp. 404–22, 407.

23 Luther, *Commentary on Psalm 110* (cited in Voss, *Priesthood of All Believers*, Kindle Location 4715).

24 Cara Lovell has recently argued persuasively that both the 'subjective' discernment of the individual and the 'objective' discernment of the Church are needed, with greater emphasis being placed on the latter ('"Do you Believe that God is Calling You to this Ministry?" Subjective and Objective Factors in Discerning Vocation in the Church of England', *Theology and Ministry* 6 (2020), pp. 62–88).

3

Clerics and Anti-clericalism

If we are left to devise our own structuring for the communal organism of the Church, if this is a matter incidental or indifferent for the real identity and integrity of the Body, does this not suggest that there is, so to speak, some bit of our unreconstructed individual ego-existence that remains untouched by incorporation into Christ ... If the Church is essentially an undifferentiated community of mutual service, gathered from time to time for a visibly united act of worship, does this not weaken the strong Pauline sense of sharply distinct charisms, gifts which give the community a concrete shape? Mutuality in the Church is not simply a relation between abstract persons, whose identities are interchangeable; nor does a theology of charisms in the Church simply mean that everybody has something generally useful to offer, depending on their temperament ... To be in the Church at all is to be the recipient of some sort of charism, some place to occupy, not because the community decides that a job needs doing but because God knows what the community will need. (Rowan Williams[1])

How did the Church overcome its reticence to use the term 'priest' of a Christian minister? In the last two chapters we saw how the New Testament ascribed the language and conceptual framework of priesthood to Christ individually and to the Church corporately. We saw too how Luther restated this corporate 'priesthood of all believers' in the face of what he saw to be corruption in the medieval priesthood. In this chapter, we consider how and why it was that the term 'priest' became associated with the ministerial priesthood at all. We do so not to prioritize the ordained ministry of priests over other forms of ministry and especially over other forms of ordained ministry such as deacon or bishop. Rather, we trace this evolution of language to begin tracing a theology of Christian ministry, including ordained ministry and priesthood, which returns more closely to Christ's priesthood as foundational. Finally, we turn to consider how the exercise of particular ordained ministries might help the whole Church to flourish in their particular callings to share in Christ's universal priesthood.

A Christian priesthood?

As we've seen, the New Testament does not ascribe the language of 'priesthood' to particular Christian individuals. Priestly and high priestly motifs are applied to Christ, and the letter to the Hebrews is explicit that Christ is our high priest. Priestly language is used only of Christians corporately in 1 Peter and the book of Revelation. Christians are called to be 'a chosen race' and 'a royal priesthood'.

It is usually noted that the Church demonstrates a huge reticence in applying the language of the cultic priesthood to any individual calling or ministry, particularly avoiding use of the term '*hiereus*'. Instead, we find a variety of individual ministries on the pages of our New Testament. These include the familiar overseer (*episcopos*, from which we get our term 'bishop'), elder or presbyter (*presbuteros*, from which we get our term 'priest') and deacon (*diakonos*).

However, the gradual application of priestly language to individual Christian ministers can be seen to be a trend that begins at a time when writings that made their way into our New Testament were also being written. Hank Voss decries this trend as a 'defrocking' of the common royal priesthood of every Christian.[2] However, we shall argue that rather than being a defrocking (a removing of priestly status) the discovery of particular ministerial priesthoods and ordained callings serves to enable rather than diminish the priestly calling of all Christians.

The first example of priestly language being used to describe Christian ministries can be found in the text *1 Clement*. This text is generally ascribed to Clement of Rome writing in the year AD 96 but unlike some other texts written in or around this time it does not make it into our biblical canon. In Hebrews, we saw the author's argumentative step in establishing Christ's priesthood through Jesus' humanity, so it is perhaps interesting that in Clement we can observe a similar, albeit more restrictive, nod towards the shared ancestry of Jesus and the Levitical priesthood. Clement notes that Abraham is a common ancestor both to Christ and the Levitical priesthood.[3] Clement is clear that Christ's priesthood is primary: 'He is the High Priest of all our offerings, the defender and helper of our infirmity. By Him we look up to the heights of heaven. By Him we behold, as in a glass, His immaculate and most excellent visage. By Him are the eyes of our hearts opened' (*1 Clement* 36).

However, in the context of division in the Corinthian Church which resulted in the deposition of some of their elders and overseers, Clement appeals to the divine ordering of the cultic priesthood to establish the divine appointment of particular Christian ministries: 'For his own peculiar services are assigned to the high priest, and their own proper place is prescribed to the priests, and their own special ministrations devolve on the Levites. The layman is bound by the laws that pertain to laymen' (*1 Clement* 40). As Voss notes: 'Clement is the first in extant Greek literature to use λαϊκός in a religious sense, suggesting two ranks (τάγματι) among believers.'[4]

In doing so, Clement introduces a lay/clerical distinction into Christian theology that, as we shall see, is deeply misleading as it causes us to focus on what is ultimately an irrelevant binary in the face of the multiplicity of particular callings and ministries, lay and ordained. This is not to say clerical and lay callings are not different, not least in the sense that every calling is distinct. While they are different, one or other is not better. Clement introduces this distinction in order to restore order into a divided community. We see that one of the consequences of the particular orders of ministry is designed to be a unity that enables each to flourish. However, all too often this order itself is prioritized at the expense of the flourishing of *all* believers this order is designed to promote. Christian 'order' gets itself into a muddle, which robs each vocation of the equality of status, when it promotes the status of clerical callings above other callings. Diversity of particularity of calling does not mean a diversity of status or prestige.

While stopping short of using the language of cultic priesthood for individuals within the Christian community, Clement makes a parallel between the cultic priesthood and Christian ministry. He implies the limitation of the cultic priesthood to those descended from Aaron was to prevent the kind of dispute that had arisen in Corinth (*1 Clement* 43). He goes on to claim that the appointment of particular ministers to oversee the community in the apostles' wake was likewise because the apostles foreknew that disputes would arise, therefore they established a line of succession (*1 Clement* 44). It's important to note that this line of succession is not based on a particular earthly lineage but suitable candidates with the consent of the whole Church.

Here we see the foundations of what is sometimes called 'apostolic succession' – the continuation of ministries from one generation to a next via particular bishops in what's often referred to as 'the historic episcopate'. This would later be formalized by the 'laying on of hands'. For Clement, this form of succession is designed to prevent dissension in the Christian community. In our time it is perhaps more often a source of dispute between churches as to whether they truly stand in this apostolic line. For example, discussion between the Methodists and the Church of England about closer collaboration often hinges on the Methodists regularizing their patterns of ministry to be brought in line with the essential Anglican understanding of how ministerial oversight is exercised within this apostolic inheritance. We see here that this succession is intended to liberate Christian community from discord which enables the flourishing of the particularity of callings.

Rowan Williams notes that some sort of concept of 'apostolic succession' within how Churches are ordered does offer liberative potential for all Christian callings. In what might be descried as a lived example of 'apostolic succession', Williams draws on the example of one of his predecessors as Archbishop of Canterbury – Michael Ramsey – to suggest that something like apostolic succession frees the Church from a certain kind of human focus that distorts the Church by moving focus away from Christ's desire for the Church and puts *our* desire for the Church to be this or that at the centre:

> The lack of a theology of the apostolic role leaves a gap in the area of the concrete historical givenness of the Church which seems to suggest that there is a whole dimension of the Church's life that is after all amenable to human choice, to a process of devising structures that will function as we want them to ... Ramsey [in *The Gospel and the Catholic Church*] is in effect saying that justification by faith really requires something like apostolic succession if it is not to slip into fresh distortion.[5]

The apostolic inheritance that Clement points to as a basis for church order also helps us to see that the particularity of individual calling is not isolated from the calling of the entire Christian community.[6] Each calling builds on and bequeaths to those who have gone before us and will follow us in the Christian faith. This pattern of inheriting and bequeathing is an essential feature of each of our particular callings. It should therefore come as no surprise that this pattern finds its basis in Scripture: 'I hand on to you what I first received.'[7]

Clement stops short of applying the language of priesthood to individuals. His comparison of Christian ministry with the cultic priesthood sets in train a trend towards the description of particular forms of Christian ministry as 'priesthood'. His legacy is positive in recognizing the importance of order to enable the flourishing of each and every vocation. The contextual focus of his letter, on enabling the flourishing of the particular ministry of the elders and overseers in the context of dispute, means that his focus on these particular ministries introduces an ultimately unhelpful binary between clergy and laity. We now turn to see how the application of the language of priesthood directly to Christian individuals might better serve this flourishing of the particular calling of each member of the Church.

The term 'priest' (*hiereus* (Greek) or *sacerdos* (Latin)) is first used of a Christian in relation to the ministry of bishop and is seen in the early part of the third century AD. The term 'bishop' is, as we saw above, derived from the Greek '*episcopos*' which refers to the ministry of 'oversight'. It's widely argued that Tertullian (*c.* AD 160–225) is the first to use the term 'priest' to describe the ministry of bishop. Tertullian was from Carthage in North Africa and is often credited as being the first substantial theologian writing in Latin. It's also significant that he is the first to associate the ministry of presbyters and deacons with the language of 'priestly' ministry. While Tertullian's usage is the first extant evidence for the use of such language to describe the Christian ministry, Colin Bulley notes that: 'the fact that Tertullian makes such priestly references to the bishop and the clergy so infrequently (seven times where such a reference is very likely and three where it is less likely but quite possible) and without any apparent need to justify that usage suggests that it was well established in the North African church in Tertullian's day'.[8]

For example, Tertullian refers to the bishop as 'chief priest' (*summus sacerdos*) in the context of disputes concerning the sacrament of baptism and with reference to the order of precedence in terms of who baptizes others:

> the chief priest (who is the bishop) has the right: in the next place, the presbyters and deacons, yet not without the bishop's authority, on account of the honour of the Church, which being preserved, peace is preserved. Beside these, even

laymen have the right; for what is equally received can be equally given. Unless bishops, or priests, or deacons, be on the spot, other disciples are called i.e. to the work.[9]

For our purposes, it's important to note here that this first use of the language of '*sacerdos*' or 'priest' of an individual both associates that language with the flourishing of all through the preservation of order to avoid dissension (as we saw also in *1 Clement*) but also that the bishop's calling to this particular priestly ministry is not divorced from the general priesthood of the baptized. However, each of these callings is particular and brings with it an allotted set of tasks by virtue of that calling depending, in this case, on who else is present in the circumstances.

Elsewhere, Tertullian uses priestly language not only of bishops, but he extends this to include the ministry of presbyters and deacons. Again, the context is significant for us here. Tertullian is writing against heretical groups who lack the particular orders of bishop, presbyter and deacon. He seems to recognize the clergy–lay distinction we encountered in *1 Clement* and applies the language of 'priestly' functions (*sacerdotalia*) to the ministry of bishops, priests and deacons in condemning the heretics' interchangeability of particular callings: 'Today one man is their bishop, tomorrow another; today he is a deacon who tomorrow is a reader; today he is a presbyter who tomorrow is a layman. For even on laymen do they impose the functions of priesthood.'[10] Bulley notes that Tertullian's use of this language without explanation or defence may suggest that it had already become commonplace within the Church in Carthage by at least the beginning of the third century AD.[11]

Cyprian of Carthage

If Tertullian is one of our earliest witnesses to the language of cultic priesthood being applied to the bishop and subsequently extended to the ordained ministry of presbyters and deacons, it is his fellow inhabitant of Carthage, Cyprian (d. AD 258), who is usually credited with establishing the application of 'priestly' language to the ministry of bishops as well as presbyters as a standard Christian use.

Cyprian regularly applies the language of the cultic priesthood (*sacerdos*) to the ministry of bishop. He also extends this language in a number of places to the ministry of presbyters. For example, he celebrates one Numidicus joining the rank of presbyters. Cyprian notes his desire that God might similarly 'adorn with glorious priests the number of our presbyters that had been desolated by the lapse of some'.[12] Elsewhere, he notes how 'presbyters are associated with the bishop in priestly honour'.[13]

The contexts in which the language of cultic priesthood is applied to the ministry of bishops and subsequently presbyters are significant for our purposes – namely, its association with the celebration of the Eucharist and in the context of the practice of reconciliation. Reconciliation is itself associated with the Eucharist as the reconciled sinner is permitted to participate once again in the celebration of the Eucharist having been reconciled to the community, or rather had the reconciliation recognized by the community in the person of the bishop and subsequently presbyter.

We can see both of these applications of such language in Cyprian's famous treaty *On the Lapsed* which deals with the matter of reconciling those who had sinned by lapsing from Christian faith in a period of persecution: 'I entreat you, beloved brethren, that each one should confess his own sin, while he who has sinned is still in this world, while his confession may be received, while the satisfaction and remission made by the priests are pleasing to the Lord.'[14] Those celebrating the Eucharist and reconciling sinners are referred to as priests and sacrificial language is applied to the Eucharist (even in the context of a letter dealing with the pagan sacrifices of which some of the lapsed had partaken or considered during the persecution).

This connection of priesthood and Eucharist is made even more strongly in a significant letter in which Cyprian writes to one Caecilius condemning the practice of some who had begun replacing the wine of the Eucharist with water. Cyprian bases his argument here on the institution of the Eucharist as a command of the Lord: 'do this in memory of me' (Luke 22.19; 1 Corinthians 11.24). Cyprian insists that those who use water 'by human and novel institution depart from that which Christ our Master both prescribed and did'.[15]

In relation to the Eucharist, Cyprian describes Jesus as the 'teacher and founder of this sacrifice'.[16] Throughout the letter, the priesthood of Jesus is primary. In a section that draws on the Melchizedek imagery from Hebrews we encountered above, he writes: 'who is more a priest of the most high God than our Lord Jesus Christ, who offered a sacrifice to God the Father'.[17] The cultic imagery of 'sacrifice' is applied to the Eucharist but, again significantly, this sacrifice is consistently related to Jesus' saving passion and death: 'the blood of Christ is not offered if there be no wine in the cup, nor the Lord's sacrifice celebrated with a legitimate consecration unless our oblation and sacrifice respond to His passion'.[18] He makes this identification even clearer later in the same letter: 'we make mention of His passion in all sacrifices (for the Lord's passion is the sacrifice which we offer)'.[19]

Cyprian recognizes that it is from Christ's primary priesthood that flows the priestly ministry of particular individuals within the ministry of the Church:

For if Jesus Christ, our Lord and God, is Himself the chief priest of God the Father, and has first offered Himself a sacrifice to the Father, and has commanded this to be done in commemoration of Himself, certainly that priest truly discharges the office of Christ, who imitates that which Christ did; and he then offers a true and full sacrifice in the Church to God the Father, when he proceeds to offer it according to what he sees Christ Himself to have offered.[20]

We witness in this letter references to the cultic imagery of priesthood being applied both to the celebration of the Eucharist within the Church, but also significantly to Christ's action at the Last Supper. This connection is vital. For our purposes it's important to note that the language of priesthood here is particularly associated with the celebration of the Eucharist because of the Eucharist's connection with the events of Christ's saving passion and death. This cultic language of 'sacrifice' is rightly applied to the Eucharist not because a particular celebration of the Eucharist is a fresh priestly sacrifice to God, but because every Eucharist unites us to Christ's passion and is therefore a share in the one sacrifice of Christ for us.[21]

Jaroslav Pelikan notes that the use of the language of the cultic priesthood in this way 'shows how independent Christian doctrine had become of its Jewish origins and how free it felt to appropriate terms and concepts from the Jewish tradition despite its earlier disparagement of them'.[22] There is an irony here. Part of the reason that Cyprian and others are able to draw on the cultic language of 'priesthood' so freely is because of the Church's recognition of the Christian Old Testament as Scripture. Much of Cyprian's argument in his letter to Caecilius draws on examples from the Old Testament. However, he does so not to re-establish the former cultic priesthood but to draw the connection ever more strongly between the Christian priestly ministry of celebrating the Eucharist and the sacrifice of Christ himself once offered.

Priests *for* all priests: Eucharist and reconciliation

> Formed by the word, they are to call their hearers to repent-
> ance and to declare in Christ's name the absolution and for-
> giveness of their sins ... they are to preside at the Lord's table
> and lead his people in worship, offering with them a spiritual
> sacrifice of praise and thanksgiving.[23]

Cyprian's witness is significant because he uses the cultic language of 'priesthood' in a way that establishes this terminology
as standard for bishops and presbyters. He does so in a way
that is resolutely focused on Christ's priesthood, but also sets
the context for understanding the particularity of the ministry
of bishops and presbyters.

The emergence of the application of cultic priestly language
to those who exercise the ministry of bishop and presbyter is
significant. It clarifies, and gives insight to, a trajectory that
emerges from the time of the writing of the New Testament (as
we saw in *1 Clement*) that focuses attention via the Eucharist
on the sacrifice of Christ on the cross and the commandment
of Christ to 'do this in memory of him'. The institution (and
subsequent celebrations) of the Eucharist and Christ's death
on the cross cannot – as we saw above – be separated as it is
through Christ's priestly act in the institution of the Eucharist that renders the actions of those who would put him to
death as, ultimately, futile. Without the events that surround
his death, particularly the institution of the Eucharist, Christ
would be victim but not priest. Without his death on the cross,
Christ may have been priest but not victim. Whereas some
modern theology has a tendency to emphasize this victimhood ('he died for us'), we see in the New Testament that it
is essential to recognize Christ as both victim *and* priest. This
combination underlines that it was Christ who died for us; the
initiative was, and is always, God's.

The particular calling of priestly ministry is eucharistic. It
draws attention to Christ's priestly act at the Last Supper and
his sacrificial act on the cross, and it holds before the entire

community that this priesthood and victimhood of Christ are one and the same. It is therefore important to recognize that the ordained priesthood is grounded on the particular exercise of Christ's priesthood and not the analogy to cultic priesthood. Rather than being a priesthood that takes life in a cultic sense, it is a priesthood that enables life through its proximity to vulnerability and Christ's action of 'binding himself to vulnerability before he is bound (literally) by human violence'.[24] All Christian life and priesthood is therefore a kind of laying down of life in service in order to take up the particular shape of life to which God is calling *you*. This is what it means to exist as Church, that 'differentiated fellowship of complementary gifts and "positionings"'[25] in which some would be apostles, some prophets, some evangelists, some pastors and teachers, to equip the saints for the work of ministry, for building up the body of Christ (Ephesians 4.11–12) and which requires some to take up the particular role of the ordained.

The eucharistic shape of Christian priesthood is reflected both in the particular calling to have a specific role in relation to celebration of the Eucharist and in the ministry of reconciliation. Reconciliation is both the formal pronouncement of absolution and the wider set of pastoral tasks shared with other particular callings. Pronouncing absolution is itself a eucharistic act as it includes the restoration of the reconciled sinner into the eucharistic assembly and life of the community. The ministry of bishops as overseers is primarily a ministry of oversight of those who are to take on this role in relation to the Eucharist and formal absolution. The sphere of particularity in this calling to ordained priesthood is perhaps small. However, as both eucharistic presidency and the proclamation of absolution constitute positions of power within the Church it is perhaps this reason that led to these ministries being associated with the call to eldership and oversight. In relation to the Eucharist, power is held through the potential of becoming a misplaced focus of attention and in relation to reconciliation, power is held through the potential misuse of authority in pronouncing or delaying reconciliation.

It is for these reasons that we shall see that intentionality is an essential feature for how Christian priesthood is lived out to avoid the potential for clericalist abuse of these particular callings. This intentionality has been nourished by a set of tools in the celebration of the Eucharist which are helpful aids to the entire Christian life. It is also why focus on Christ's priesthood is particularly essential for the exercise of the particular calling to Christian priesthood. By grounding ordained priesthood in Christ's priesthood we are ever reminded that the reconciliation we recognize is not as a result of our absolution but by Christ's action on the cross. By focusing on Christ's priestly action at the Last Supper, we make him the proper focus and summit of attention in our eucharistic celebrations.

Inhabited in this way, the particular calling to ordained ministry serves the particular calling of all those who share in Christ's priesthood – that is, all Christians. Indeed, this is the very calling to ordained ministry, as reflected in the World Council of Churches' *Baptism, Eucharist and Ministry*:

> Ordained ministers are related, as are all Christians, both to the priesthood of Christ, and to the priesthood of the Church. But they may appropriately be called priests because they fulfil a particular priestly service by strengthening and building up the royal and prophetic priesthood of the faithful through word and sacraments.[26]

The calling to enable the royal priesthood of the entire Church through focus on Christ's own act of priesthood in the Last Supper is essential to the life of the ordained. The particular calling to ordained priesthood nourishes the priesthood of all believers through these acts of a particular role in the eucharistic celebration and realizing of the forgiveness of sins. As we shall see in Chapter 6 below, the ministry of deacons is itself priestly in a different way through a different particularity of calling and ministry that is no less (and arguably considerably more) vital for the Church's enabling of the priesthood of all Christians. The diaconate is a form of 'reconciliation' or healing of the Church's centre, which is essential for overcoming the potential for clericalism in every walk of the Church's life. The connection of the ordained priesthood to Christ's priestly act in the Last Supper generally and in the Eucharist in particular is vital for the potential for priestly ministry to realize its vocation as an antidote to clericalism, through its embodiment of the particularity of calling and its refocusing, through the ministry of Eucharist and reconciliation, on the saving acts of God in Christ. However, even this ministry itself requires persistent refocusing to overcome the potential for clericalism. The Western liturgy of the Eucharist has developed a particular series of tools to keep the intention and focus squarely on Christ throughout. These tools are perhaps little known outside of certain contexts and are the subject of our next chapter.

Priestly ministry therefore derives its particularity within the ministry of the Church not from the cultic imagery of the Levitical priesthood itself but from the action and initiative of Christ in his commandment to 'do this' and in his saving passion and death. The priestly act of Christ in the institution of the Eucharist inaugurates this new priesthood. The cultic imagery of priesthood is appropriate for this Christian priestly ministry because it serves to illuminate Christ's action at the Last Supper and on the cross, as we saw in the previous chapter. This connection needs to be constantly at the focus of priestly and ordained ministry. The potential for clericalism is rife when the cultic imagery of the priesthood – with an associated qualifying elite – is at the root of Christian priestly ministry and not the priestly act of identification and renunciation we witnessed as being the grounds of Christ's priesthood at the Last Supper.

Notes

1 Rowan Williams, *Ramsey Lecture, Durham – 'The Lutheran Catholic'* (2004), available at: http://rowanwilliams.archbishopofcanterbury.org/articles.php/2102/ramsey-lecture-durham-the-lutheran-catholic.html [accessed 10.09.2021].

2 Hank Voss, *The Priesthood of All Believers and the Missio Dei: A Canonical, Catholic, and Contextual Perspective* (Eugene, OR: Pickwick), Kindle Location 3920.

3 *1 Clement* 32, available at: www.newadvent.org/fathers/1010.htm [accessed 10.09.2021].

4 Voss, *Priesthood of All Believers*, Kindle Location 3957.

5 Williams, 'Lutheran Catholic'. See Michael Ramsey, *The Gospel and the Catholic Church* (1936) (second edition, London: Longmans, 1955).

6 Ramsey notes similarly: 'the self is known in its reality as a self when it ceases to be solitary and learns its utter dependence, and the "individuality" of Christians, with all its rich variety, springs from the death and resurrection in the Body which is one' (Ramsey, *Gospel and the Catholic Church*, p. 38).

7 1 Corinthians 15.3; cf. 1 Corinthians 11.23.

8 Colin Bulley, 'From General Priesthood to Special Priesthood: Development in the Christian Literature of the First Three Centuries' (PhD University of Edinburgh, 1993), p. 92, available at: https://era.ed.ac.uk/handle/1842/20354 [accessed 13.09.2021]. See also Colin Bulley, *The Priesthood of Some Believers: Developments from the General to the Special Priesthood in the Christian Literature of the First Three Centuries* (Milton Keynes: Paternoster, 2000).

9 Tertullian, *On Baptism* 17, available at: www.newadvent.org/fathers/0321.htm [accessed 13.09.2021].

10 Tertullian, *Prescription Against Heretics* 41, available at: www.newadvent.org/fathers/0311.htm [accessed 13.09.2021].

11 Bulley, *From General Priesthood*, p. 88. He notes further: this use of language is not limited to the Latin-speaking tradition. Bulley explores the possibility of Hippolytus (*c.* AD 170–236) making use of the equivalent Greek terms for 'priest' (*hiereus*) at around the same time: 'Hippolytus, then, was very happy to use high priestly terminology of the bishop, and saw no need to justify it, suggesting, as with Tertullian, that it was a generally accepted usage. He also regarded presbyters as part of the priesthood' (*From General Priesthood*, p. 99). Many of these references occur in his *Apostolic Tradition*, a text whose attribution to Hippolytus is now disputed.

12 Cyprian, *Epistle 34*, available at: www.newadvent.org/fathers/
050634.htm [accessed 15.09.2021]. Note that the numbering of Cyprian's epistles varies; Bulley cites these and that below as Epistle 40 and
61 respectively.

13 Cyprian, *Epistle 57*, available at: www.newadvent.org/fathers/
050657.htm [accessed 16.09.2021].

14 Cyprian, *On the Lapsed* 29, available at: www.newadvent.org/
fathers/050703.htm [accessed 17.09.2021].

15 Cyprian, *Epistle 62.1 (To Caecilius)*, available at: www.newad
vent.org/fathers/050662.htm [accessed 16.09.2021].

16 Cyprian, *Epistle 62.1.*

17 Cyprian, *Epistle 62.4.*

18 Cyprian, *Epistle 62.9.*

19 Cyprian, *Epistle 62.17.*

20 Cyprian, *Epistle 62.14.*

21 For the use of 'sacrifice' as an apt metaphor for the Eucharist,
see especially Rowan Williams, *Eucharistic Sacrifice: The Roots of a
Metaphor* (Bramcote: Grove Books, 1982) and Colin Buchanan (ed.),
Essays on Eucharistic Sacrifice in the Early Church (Bramcote: Grove
Books, 1984).

22 Jaroslav Pelikan, *The Emergence of the Catholic Tradition (100–
600)* (London: University of Chicago Press, 1975), p. 26.

23 The Archbishops' Council, *Common Worship: Ordination Services* (London: Church House Publishing, 2007), available at: www.
churchofengland.org/prayer-and-worship/worship-texts-and-resources/
common-worship/ministry/common-worship-ordination-0 [accessed 22.
06.2014].

24 Rowan Williams, 'Sacraments of the New Society' in Rowan
Williams, *On Christian Theology* (Oxford: Blackwell, 2000), p. 216.

25 Williams, *'Lutheran Catholic'.*

26 *Baptism, Eucharist, and Ministry* (Geneva: World Council of
Churches, 1982), p. 20, available at: www.anglicancommunion.org/
media/102580/lima_document.pdf [accessed 17.09.2021].

4

Worship and Priesthood

When the priest has her back to the people, it is symbolically
clear that she is adopting the position of 'offering' on behalf
of the laity: she is facing Godwards, representing the *laos* ...
but when she turns around, whether to greet (at the sursum
corda), or to offer the consecrated elements, or to bless, she
has moved to the other side of the divide, representing Christ,
offering God to the people – again, in the terms of the nuptial
metaphor, both summoning and destabilizing the 'masculine'
posture of the bridegroom's self-gift. Without these bodily
reversals and movements in the liturgy, I suggest, something
deeply significant to the enactment of this destabilization is
lost. (Sarah Coakley[1])

How does the particular ministry of those called to serve as
ordained presbyters or 'priests' avoid the potential for clericalism which is hazardously close in any exercise of this calling?
We saw above that the defining priestly acts of eucharistic
presidency and pronouncing absolution are both fraught with
the potential for clericalist misuses of position and power.
Far from enabling the priestly people of God from inhabiting
their particular calling, the exercise of the particular calling
to ordained priesthood can often be exercised in a way that
diminishes rather than enables these callings.

In this chapter, we consider gifts that have emerged within
the celebration of the Eucharist in the Western tradition that
help us all in our particular vocation.[2] These help the president
especially to keep her focus fixed decisively on Christ. This
intentionality and resolute focus on Christ provides one of the

surest antidotes to clericalism – where focus is truly on Christ the potential for the clericalist focus to shift to this or that individual or group is diminished.

If a certain relationship to the Eucharist is one of the distinctive marks of the shape of priestly calling, namely the 'presidency' of the eucharistic assembly, it's perhaps a surprise that the Eucharist can all too easily become a perfunctory aspect of the priest's calling. Even the Eucharist, the 'source and summit of the Christian life', can all too easily become another activity or task to be done. Those ordained priest are especially prone to fall into the habit of letting worship, particularly celebration of the Eucharist, become a work to be worked, rather than a prayer to be prayed. This is not just a danger for clergy, but for every Christian. We attend church. We worship. We tick the box. We get on with our lives, which may remain more or less unchanged. Our prayer life, once on fire with an awareness of the presence of God, gets stale over time.

Within the Eucharist, certain prayers have developed in the Western tradition during the course of the liturgy that offer an antidote to the ever-present danger of worship becoming another 'thing' to do in the Christian life. These prayers are said silently or in an inaudible voice at certain points of the liturgy and help the celebrant keep her attention focused resolutely on Christ. This resolute intention helps the celebration of the Eucharist from becoming a clericalist act in which the focus is on the celebrant. These prayers are used today within the Roman Catholic Church and some other denominations but are little known either outside of those traditions or even within those traditions as they are said so quietly as to be otherwise unheard. The purpose of this section of our exploration of priesthood is to see how these prayers offer us a rich resource for enabling the ordained priesthood to better serve its task of enabling the 'priesthood' of all believers in Christ.

These prayers are said quietly by the priest at certain points during the celebration of the Eucharist. For this reason, they are sometimes known as 'secret' prayers or, perhaps more accurately, the 'personal' prayers of the priest celebrating the Eucharist.

'Secret' prayers

Before the gospel reading: (blessing of a deacon) 'May the Lord be in your heart and on your lips, that you may proclaim his gospel worthily and well, in the name of the Father, and of the Son and of the Holy Spirit' and if no deacon is present, 'Cleanse my heart and my lips, almighty God, that I may worthily proclaim your holy gospel.'

At the end of the gospel reading: 'Through the words of the gospel may our sins be wiped away.'

While preparing the communion chalice: 'By the mystery of this water and wine may we come to share in the divinity of Christ who humbled himself to share in our humanity.'

Before the consecration of bread and wine: 'With humble spirit and contrite heart may we be accepted by you, O Lord, and may our sacrifice in your sight this day be pleasing to you, Lord God.'

Cleaning hands before consecration (known as 'lavabo'): 'Wash me, O Lord, from my iniquity and cleanse me from my sin.'

After consecration, mixing a small piece of consecrated bread with consecrated wine (known as 'fermentum'): 'May this mingling of the Body and Blood of our Lord Jesus Christ bring eternal life to us who receive it.'

After the Agnus Dei (Lamb of God): 'Lord Jesus Christ, Son of the living God, who, by the will of the Father and the work of the Holy Spirit, through your Death gave life to the world, free me by this, your most holy Body and Blood, from all my sins and from every evil; keep me always faithful to your commandments, and never let me be parted from you' or 'May the receiving of your Body and Blood, Lord Jesus Christ, not bring me to judgment and condemnation, but through your loving mercy be for me protection in mind and body and a healing remedy.'

Before receiving communion: 'May the Body of Christ keep me safe for eternal life' and 'May the Blood of Christ keep me safe for eternal life.'

Washing the communion vessels (the ablutions): 'What has passed our lips as food, O Lord, may we possess in purity of heart, that what has been given to us in time may be our healing for eternity.'

These prayers are private insofar as they are said quietly and not addressed to the congregation as a whole. However, they are not intended to be secret. Wider knowledge of them can help every Christian engage more prayerfully with the Eucharist. These prayers help us pray as we do the work of the liturgy as the body of Christ.

These prayers also demonstrate the truth of another prayerful catchphrase, '*lex orandi, lex credendi*' ('what is prayed is what is believed' or 'the rule of praying is the rule of belief'). They help us to understand theologically some of what is happening in the prayers that make up the liturgy of the Eucharist. They help us better to understand theologically what we believe to be happening to us as a worshipping community in the course of the liturgy, as well as keeping our focus, especially the focus of the celebrating priest, on that worship and resolutely on Christ throughout.

These prayers help us keep our focus not only on worshipping rather than working, but they also sharpen our focus on the object of our worship: Christ himself. They help us to focus on what he has done, that which we celebrate in every Eucharist; what he is doing even now in the course of this Eucharist; and what we pray he might do in the future for all of those present and for whom we pray.

The prayers that are said quietly by the celebrant occur at

key moments in the liturgy: at the proclamation of the gospel; the preparation of the gifts of bread and wine; after the consecration; at the point of receiving communion; and during the ablutions as the vessels used during the Eucharist are cleansed. Some of these prayers are proper to the ministry of deacons, which we will explore in our next chapter, but are said by the priest where there is no deacon present. We will explore both these prayers here, while making clear which are in keeping with the deacon's role in the liturgy within the Western liturgical tradition.

Proclaiming the gospel

The first such prayer is a prayer of preparation before proclaiming the gospel. If a deacon is present, the celebrant blesses her or him with the prayer: 'May the Lord be in your heart and on your lips, that you may proclaim his gospel worthily and well, in the name of the Father, and of the Son and of the Holy Spirit.'

If there is no deacon, the priest says quietly to herself: 'Cleanse my heart and my lips, almighty God, that I may worthily proclaim your holy gospel.'

The blessing of the deacon is a prayer that the deacon might read the gospel in a manner befitting the content of the gospel he or she is about to proclaim. Likewise, the priest prays that he or she might worthily proclaim the gospel. It's easy to mistake this prayer for a professionalism that would indicate something of the clericalism such prayers are intended to help to avoid – that the reader might do a good job. However, the words used are more profound. This is a prayer for personal transformation that enables the priest or deacon to witness to the Lord more clearly, not only by reading the gospel but showing forth that gospel by a conversion of the heart. 'May the Lord be in your heart', 'may my heart be cleansed'.

We see here how these prayers help snap us out of worshipping in a perfunctory or professional way. This isn't just a prayer to do a job well. This is a prayer for complete personal transformation that means our celebration of the liturgy will overflow from the transformation of our lives. That the celebrant and those present will live out their particular calling to the particular transformation of life that to which they are being called by God.

The scriptural resonances in these prayers here are rich. The prayer combines imagery from the psalms and elsewhere in Scripture which call on God to cleanse the heart and lips of the speaker. For example, the cry of the psalmist in Psalm 51 that their iniquity might be washed away, and their lips opened to declare the Lord's praise. We are reminded too of the cleansing of the prophet Isaiah's lips before being sent to proclaim God's message. Our second prayer comes at the end of the gospel. Once the gospel has been proclaimed, he or she kisses the gospel book and says quietly: 'through the words of the gospel may our sins be wiped away'.

This prayer enters the liturgy around the year 1000. The kiss that precedes it stresses our intimacy with and devotion towards the gospel as we proclaim it. This kiss unites those lips that have just proclaimed the gospel message to the words of the gospel on the page. As we were reminded of the extent of personal transformation called for in our first prayer, so too in this act. We unite the whole of ourselves to the gospel and pray that the whole of our selves might be transformed through the gospel we proclaim.

Below we shall consider the relationship of the ordained priesthood to the ordained diaconate. While not a formal prayer of absolution, that this prayer is a petition for absolution, said by a deacon, is significant as a reminder of the 'priestliness' of the ministry of the order of deacons. Rather, it is a reminder that deacons share in the priesthood of Christ in their particular calling to ministry no less than those who are called to the ordained priesthood.

This prayer associated with the kissing of the gospel book itself might initially strike us as odd. How do these words atone for sin? How does proclaiming the gospel wipe away our sin? It is not the particular words themselves that effect the forgiveness of sin, but the forgiveness of sin that is at the heart of the message of the gospel we proclaim. It is not the words themselves, but the gospel of redemption to which they attest that wipes away our sin. We are reminded that the gospel we proclaim is the gospel of Jesus Christ, whom we encounter as we proclaim the gospel in the liturgy, who has put away our sin.

Preparing the table

Our next prayer occurs as the bread and the wine are prepared. Preparation is an important part of every Eucharist. Such preparation helps cultivate the intentionality of focus on Christ and the exercise of a particular calling which is vital in overcoming the patterns of clericalism. Preparation in worship is not just something that's an important part of worship for those leading worship but those who will worship through the worship leading of others. We are preparing ourselves for an encounter with Christ.

In the context of the liturgy of the Eucharist, we are preparing ourselves for a particularly intimate encounter as we receive God's gift of God's self to us in bread and wine, as we share in the body and blood of the Eucharist. Just as we prepare ourselves carefully before and in the course of the liturgy for this encounter, by meditating on God's word, by confessing our sins. So too the bread and wine are prepared, the 'elements' of this sacramental encounter.

This prayer of preparation is said by a deacon if present. As the deacon or priest prepares the wine to be consecrated, they add a small amount of water to the wine while saying quietly: 'by the mystery of this water and wine may we come to share in the divinity of Christ who humbled himself to share in our humanity'.

The use of the word 'mystery' here points forward to the 'sacrament' that is about to take place. The Latin *sacramentum* was used in the Latin Vulgate translation of the New Testament to render the Greek *mysterion*. This reminds us of the element of mystery in each sacramental encounter with God. We do not completely understand the sacramental transformation of bread and wine about to take place, nor the transformation they will effect in us. As the prayer continues, just as there is an element of 'mystery' in each and every sacrament, we are reminded of the mysterious uniting of humanity and divinity in Christ. The prayer recalls the mystery of the incarnation, and the saving purpose of that mystery.

In the second century, St Irenaeus famously noted the effect of the unity of human and divine in Christ for our salvation in his *Against Heresies*: 'our Lord Jesus Christ, who did, through His transcendent love, become what we are, that He might bring us to be even what He is Himself'. Later, in the fourth century, St Athanasius reflects in his *On the Incarnation* on the consequences of the incarnation for our salvation: 'For He was made man that we might be made God' (54.3). Such theologies refer to our 'divinization' or 'theosis' in Christ. They find their basis in the hope described at 2 Peter 1.4 that we 'may become participants in the divine nature'.

This association with the preparation of the chalice is both a reminder of the unity with God we experience as we participate in this sacrament, that our communion is not only with one another but with him who calls us to celebrate this sacrament. We are reminded of the unity with Christ that we enjoy as we share in his body.

The prayer itself is found as an early Christmas collect, reflecting its focus on the incarnation, in the Leonine Sacramentary – an early liturgical source from the sixth century. It first enters the liturgy in association with the preparation of the chalice at the end of the first millennium.

This is not the only prayer that has been associated with the mixing of water and wine at this point. Other prayers have stressed the symbolism of water and wine as representative of the blood and water that flows from Christ's side as he is pierced on the cross (John 19.34; also 1 John 5.6). While no explicit reference remains in the prayer as we have it today, the mixing of water and wine points forward to that blood and water and to the cross from which they flow.

In the treatise on the Eucharist we encountered above, Cyprian reflects on the mixing of water and wine in the chalice as a symbol of Christian unity:

> we see that in the water is understood the people, but in the wine is showed the blood of Christ. But when the water is mingled in the cup with wine, the people is made one with Christ, and the assembly of believers is associated and conjoined with Him on whom it believes ... Thus the cup of the Lord is not indeed water alone, nor wine alone, unless each be mingled with the other; just as, on the other hand, the body of the Lord cannot be flour alone or water alone, unless both should be united and joined together and compacted in the mass of one bread; in which very sacrament our people are shown to be made one, so that in like manner as many grains, collected, and ground, and mixed together into one mass, make one bread; so in Christ, who is the heavenly bread, we may know that there is one body, with which our number is joined and united.[3]

In this single prayer and its associated action, the themes of incarnation and salvation are also united. The words of the prayer call to mind the incarnation, the mixing of water and wine symbolize the crucifixion, all in preparation for the sacrament we are about to celebrate. We are reminded that these are all united in our Eucharist. We celebrate his birth as one of us in every Eucharist. We call to mind the Lord's death at every Eucharist. In every Eucharist we are united to both as we are united to him.

Before consecration

The next personal prayer of the celebrant is a prayer said on behalf of all those about to share in the celebration of the Eucharist. The celebrant bows while saying quietly: 'With humble spirit and contrite heart may we be accepted by you, O Lord, and may our sacrifice in your sight this day be pleasing to you, Lord God'. This prayer enters the liturgy in the ninth century and is based on the longer form of Daniel 3 not found in every manuscript, from the Apocryphal 'Song of the Three Children' who are placed in the fiery furnace: 'with contrite heart and humble spirit let us be received ... let our sacrifice be in your presence today and find favour before you' (3.39–40).

Much ink has been spilled about whether it is appropriate to use the metaphor of sacrifice of the celebration of the Eucharist.[4] We saw above that these associations of the Eucharist with the 'sacrifice' of Christ are the reason for the application of priestly language to those who serve as bishops and presbyters. At a basic level, in the Eucharist bread and wine are sacrificed in that they are 'set apart'. They are sanctified by being set apart as the bread and the wine of the Eucharist. The sacrifice at the heart of every Eucharist is the sacrifice that has been alluded to already in the mixing of water and wine, Christ's 'full, perfect and sufficient sacrifice, oblation and satisfaction for the sins of the world'. Christ's priestly act at the Last Supper and the intimate connection of every Eucharist with Christ's saving passion and death is primary.

Christ's sacrifice is perfect, in contrast to our own meagre attempts to set apart bread and wine within creation to fulfil his command to 'do this' in memory of him and meet him in the sacrament of his body and blood. Joseph Ratzinger (later Pope Benedict) pointed out that elsewhere in the Roman Catholic liturgy the priest prays that our Eucharist might 'be acceptable'.[5] We do not pray that our worship might be perfect as Christ's offering is perfect, but acceptable. Likewise in this personal prayer, we pray that God might 'accept' our worship. When presiding at the Eucharist, we pray that the people might encounter God not *because* of us, but *despite* us. This is an important reminder that God, not us, is to be the centre of focus as we lead worship and celebrate the Eucharist.

The humility and contrition of this prayer is *both* a reminder of the virtues that we are to cultivate at all times *and* a reflection on the limits of our own earthly capabilities to do this. Once again, these prayers are pointing us towards an entire transformation of our lives, to become those humble and contrite servants who preach the gospel in our words and deeds. We are reminded that humility and contrition are needed in the face of the flaws of our earthly lives and worship, and the potential of putting ourselves at the centre of things. We pray that God might make the best of our poor attempts to point towards him in worship, even as he transforms those very same poor attempts into places of divine encounter.

By now, it should be obvious that these prayers remind us that preparation for each Eucharist begins long before that day's celebration. They remind us to prepare constantly by cultivating our lives and being transformed by God's presence even as we celebrate that presence with us in our worship. This too is an important antidote to clericalism. The intentionality of focus on Christ and on the particular callings of all those God is calling that is required to prevent clericalist patterns of power and elevations of particular groups and elites is a constant task.

The final prayer of preparation is the lavabo, the washing of hands before the prayer of consecration of the bread and wine. The priest washes his or her hands at this point because she is about to touch the very bread of life himself once the earthly bread has been set apart for its divine purpose. The prayer that accompanies this washing is: 'wash me, O Lord, from my iniquity and cleanse me from my sin'.

This prayer is a reminder of the unworthiness of all those who preside at the Eucharist, especially those called to preside over the celebration as ordained priests. It calls to mind the sins of the celebrant and asks that they may be worthy as they approach this sacrament of encounter. The text is taken from Psalm 51.4. The practice of washing hands in preparation for the liturgy is found in our earliest liturgical sources, from the second century onwards. Once again, it is a reminder of the importance of preparation as we approach the Lord in worship.

After consecration

Once the bread and wine have been consecrated, a personal prayer accompanies the fraction, the breaking of the bread. The priest breaks the bread and deposits a small piece in the chalice of wine, while saying: 'may this mingling of the Body and Blood of our Lord Jesus Christ bring eternal life to us who receive it'. This is known as the 'fermentum', a practice that has been found in the liturgy of the Eucharist since the eighth century.

This prayer once again reminds us of the purpose of the Christian life, our salvation to life eternal. This prayer also reminds us that the bread and wine of the Eucharist are united in Christ. This is known as the 'doctrine of concomitance'. We encounter Jesus fully 'in both kinds'. We encounter Jesus fully in the bread and fully in the wine.

There is a rich symbolism of Christian unity at this point. The 'fermentum' originally constituted part of the consecrated bread sent by the bishop to other churches in the bishop's jurisdiction to symbolize the unity of the Church. It is also a reminder that the Eucharist is a share in the one sacrifice of Christ. We find such a practice from the second and third centuries. The fermentum emphasizes both the hope of eternal life proclaimed at every Eucharist, and the unity of the Church wherever the Eucharist is celebrated. The one Christ in both kinds is the one Christ present wherever the Church meets in worship.

The next personal prayer comes after the 'Agnus Dei', the communal recitation of the 'Lamb of God who takes away the sins of the world'. The priest joins hands and says: 'Lord Jesus Christ, Son of the living God, who, by the will of the Father and the work of the Holy Spirit, through your Death gave life to the world, free me by this, your most holy Body and Blood, from all my sins and from every evil; keep me always faithful to your commandments, and never let me be parted from you' or 'May the receiving of your Body and Blood, Lord Jesus Christ, not bring me to judgment and condemnation, but through your loving mercy.'

These two prayers are from the ninth and tenth centuries respectively. The latter reminds us that the Eucharist is the Church's prayer of healing par excellence. Our ultimate healing, our salvation, is found in Christ. The former is a summary of what Christ has done for all of us: freeing us from our sins and bringing life through his resurrection.

We are reminded that we do not come closer to Christ in this life than when we encounter him in this sacrament. Before receiving communion, the celebrant says quietly to themselves upon receiving the sacrament under each kind: 'May the Body of Christ keep me safe for eternal life' and 'May the Blood of Christ keep me safe for eternal life'. These prayers also emphasize the healing and protective nature of the sacrament and of our relationship to Christ and derive from the tenth century.

After communion

The final private prayer of the Eucharist is also possibly the oldest. It is found in the Leonine Sacramentary of the mid-sixth century. As the vessels that have come into contact with the consecrated bread and wine are cleaned, the priest says: 'What has passed our lips as food, O Lord, may we possess in purity of heart, that what has been given to us in time may be our healing for eternity.'

We are reminded that our true home is our eternal life in Christ. Earthly life and sustenance are not the ultimate end of our story. Our earthly life, we pray, is but the beginning of our eternal and risen life in the Christ we have encountered in this Eucharist and at every Eucharist.

This final prayer is a prayer for the transformation of life which has been at the centre of each of these prayers. We pray that we may have been cleansed and healed in our encounter with Christ in receiving the Eucharist. We are reminded that ultimate healing is not freedom from death, but through it to rise with him to eternal life. It expands our horizons from thinking this life and earthly sustenance are the ultimate bounds of our existence and encourages us to lift our gaze heavenwards to our eternal life and home. Christ has commanded us to 'do this', to celebrate the Eucharist. The Eucharist has been given to us as food for our journey as Christians and in preparation for the ultimate journey we shall one day all face. It is one of the means by which Christ delivers on his promise to be with us always, even until the end of time.

Focus

Each of these prayers helps us, whether priest or people, in our celebration of the Eucharist to open ourselves to the transforming love of God, to encounter God's transforming presence in bread and wine, and to go forth at the end of each and every Eucharist transformed and ready to help in the Church's work of transformation of the broken and divided world around us. These prayers, said quietly, and often unnoticed, by deacons and priests, have entered the Western tradition as a means to keep the focus of the deacon and priest resolutely on Christ. They help the deacon or priest to focus on Christ, and to lead others to focus on Christ through the celebration of the Eucharist. Greater knowledge and use of such prayers both by clergy and by every participant at a celebration of the Eucharist will further help to focus our hearts and minds on the Christ we serve.

This focus helps us avoid a certain clericalist mis-focus on the priest as celebrant alone (rather than on Christ as the true celebrant of every act of worship and on the celebration of the entire community gathered together in worship). Moreover, that these prayers occur at key points in the proclamation of the gospel, the preparation of the table, during the eucharistic prayer, before distributing communion, and in the cleaning of the vessels used, helps to turn these perfunctory acts into moments of divine encounter. Where proclaiming the gospel could become as much a form of focus on the person reading the gospel or the way in which the gospel reading is 'performed'

87

or cleaning the vessels could become simply a necessary task, these prayers help us to focus on Christ, and through Christ on the particular people he is calling us to be and the particular people he is calling us to serve.

There is a danger in any form of Christian worship that focus is misplaced. Whereas Christ is or was once the sole focus of our worship, we can all too easily slip into focusing more on the way we worship than the one we worship. The priest or worship leader can become the focus of our attention. Particular styles or practices can be elevated above the one to whom they are intended to lead. We can end up unintentionally worshipping our worship rather than the one whom we are intending to worship. We can end up worshipping particular ways and patterns of life – inadvertently or deliberately holding up images of the 'right' kind of person or people (who is usually the kind of person who looks like us).[6]

The potential for this focus includes the tendency recognized by Williams to exclude those 'whose history is marked down by the Church as failure, whose experience is sealed off from the exercise of "professional" pastoring'.[7] He notes that such an exercise of ministry is 'dramatically unprophetic'. A prophetic exercise of ministry is one that sees those who are currently outside the new patterns of clericalism that are emerging – the new individuals and elites that are being established within the Church. The prayers we have surveyed in this chapter are aids to the exercise of such a prophetic inhabitation of the liturgy by deacons, priests and the whole people of God. They help us to focus on Christ at each point of our communal celebration.

However, it's worth noting that there is another practice within the Western tradition that has emerged which is designed to help each participant in the eucharistic liturgy focus on Christ, and not on the celebrant of the particular person of the priest. This is the practice of presiding at the Eucharist 'facing east' or *ad orientem*. Congregations often complain that such a celebration involves the priest turning their back on the people – even if only for the short time of saying the eucharistic prayer.

The liturgical movements that climaxed in the twentieth century altered this arrangement and returned to a potentially earlier form of celebration in which the priest faced the people. This return was done for the best of intentions – to underline that the priest was no less part of the people of God than those assembled, even if the particular calling of the priest was distinct from the multitude of particular callings among those celebrating the Eucharist as a gathered congregation.

The theological significance of such a shift was to attempt to focus on the community as a whole gathered in worship, while also returning to earlier forms of gathered worship. However, this shift also brought with it unintended consequences. Far from dethroning the celebrant, celebrations of the Eucharist or acts of worship focused on the leader are often likely to make the worship leader the focus of attention. The engagement between the one presiding over worship and the gathered worshipping community can also become a form of entertainment, as the celebrant is more painfully aware of the levels of interest and attentiveness of the gathered congregation. Rather than focusing on Christ and leading others to focus on Christ with them, the focus can be on the people themselves rather than helping the people come into a transforming encounter with the Risen Lord before stepping out of the way. One of the theological gifts of eucharistic celebration 'facing East' is that priest and people are united together in facing towards God in worship. There can be clericalist 'enthronings' in such a celebration too if priests or worship leaders are set too loftily apart or professionalized too grandly away from the very people of God gathered as a whole in that place. It is not the direction we face that is the cause of such clericalism. Indeed, the tradition of priest and people facing eastwards together can be an antidote to it, as the focus on the priest can subside if they are part of a gathering focused resolutely on Christ rather than inadvertently themselves forming the centre of attention.

Sarah Coakley writes powerfully of the consequences of the priest or worship leader becoming the focus of attention in 'westward facing' celebrations of the Eucharist. She also recognizes that this propensity for the individual priest or worship leader to attract focus is radically subverted in celebration of worship when priest or leader and people *together* face a particular focus point beyond them both, as is the case in eastward celebration: 'the west-facing "stuck" position, along with the manual acts that often attend it, unnecessarily intensifies the visually "iconic" dimension of the priest's role as being *in persona Christi*; the problem then may arise for the congregation that this person's appearance (old, young, male, female, blonde, bespectacled, spotty) seems incongruous as "representative" of Christ'.[8]

I would be tempted to go further. In a priesthood that remains markedly white, straight, cis-gendered, male, able-bodied and so on, the position of the priest at the centre of attention as in westward-facing celebration risks unintentionally (or intentionally) 'enthroning' such characteristics in a decidedly clericalist way. This does not mean that eastward-facing celebration of the Eucharist or worshipping side-by-side is a guarantee of overcoming this particular clericalist pattern. However, alongside other antidotes to clericalism within the liturgy of worship more broadly, this received practice cements the position of the priest as celebrant *within* and *alongside* the community worshipping God together as a whole. Together with the aids to focus on Christ at each and every point which are the 'secret' prayers of the Western tradition, this can help the priestly presidency of the Eucharist be inhabited in a way that is decidedly anti-clericalist. Further consideration of what is truly a priestly or diaconal act that embodies the particularity of calling and what can be shared among the worshipping community as a whole further prevents the 'enthroning' of particular peoples or elites. This means that we must be attentive to the range of voices encouraged in each act of worship, the provision of legible text if we are worshipping alongside one another, the politics and theology of the worship space, what we are communicating via the use and accessibility of the building and so on. However, in so doing, we do not always need to start from scratch or reinvent the wheel so that our worship points to Christ afresh. The prayers that have been the focus of this chapter are just one example of such reflection which has extended throughout generations of those gathered in worship and has discerned various ways to keep our gaze firmly fixed not on this or that individual, grouping or clerical elite but on Christ 'the pioneer and perfecter of our faith' (Hebrews 12.2).

The celebration of the Eucharist (and the associated recognition of reconciled persons' restoration to the eucharistic community) is a defining priestly act. It is, as we have seen, through the association with the Eucharist that the imagery of 'priesthood' was first applied to Christian clergy, bishops and subsequently presbyters. It is thus central to the particular calling of priests that the Eucharist be celebrated in a way that does not elevate the status of the priestly calling to eucharistic celebration which is priesthood but points through that particular calling to Christ. Coakley describes this process as the 'mysterious liminality of priestly re-enactment'.[9] In the particular calling to eucharistic presidency, the priest becomes by God's grace 'a point of both mediation and transformation, a disturbing remaking, indeed, of the order of the world – both cosmological and personal'.[10] Such a 'remaking', focused on Christ and attentive to the patterns of clericalist elevation of groups and individuals, can flow from each and every Eucharist. Such a 'remaking' extends also to the Church which through the recognition and enabling of particular callings is ever called to reorder itself so the particular calling of each may flourish and no particular calling be elevated in status. This requires not a generalization of vocation but a renewed particularity – a particularity on who is called to what and what that particular calling means for the individual in the life of the Church. It's vital that this radical particularity (of which ordained ministry is but one sign) pays attention to God's call in the lives of even those we find the most unlikely and disturbing to our current patterns and systems of thought.

The potential for one calling or pattern of life to be established as normative is the surest path to clericalism. The ministry of deacon in the life of the Church is one of the surest defences and means of reordering the Church so that the marginalized are restored to the centre and clericalist patterns are themselves disturbed. It is that particular calling that we shall now go on to explore.

Insofar as the world is thus re-ordered, we know that the Spirit has broken in, and the Word made flesh; for what, after all, is the Incarnation itself, if not the greatest 'cosmological disturbance' that the 'world' has known?[11]

Notes

1 Sarah Coakley, 'The Woman at the Altar: Cosmological Disturbance or Gender Subversion?', *Anglican Theological Review* 86.1 (2004), pp. 75–93 (p. 89).

2 Some material in this chapter was first published on the St Mary Magdalen School of Theology blog as 'The Priest's "Secret" Prayers at Mass', available at: www.theschooloftheology.org/posts/essay/priest-secret-prayers-mass [accessed 17.09.2021].

3 Cyprian, *Epistle* 62.13.

4 See, for example, the various contributions in Colin Buchanan (ed.), *Essays on Eucharistic Sacrifice in the Early Church* (Bramcote: Grove Books, 1984).

5 Joseph Ratzinger, *Ministers of Your Joy* (Slough: St Pauls Publications, 1989), p. 21.

6 On this propensity to idolatry even in worship, see Stephen E. Fowl, *Idolatry* (Waco, TX: Baylor University Press, 2019) and Simon Cuff, *Only God Will Save Us* (London: SCM Press, 2020), pp. 114f.

7 Rowan Williams, 'Women and the Ministry: A Case for Theological Seriousness' in Monica Furlong (ed.), *Feminine in the Church* (London: SPCK, 1984), pp. 11–24 (pp. 23–4).

8 Coakley, 'Woman at the Altar', p. 90.

9 Coakley, 'Woman at the Altar', p. 93.

10 Coakley, 'Woman at the Altar', p. 93.

11 Coakley, 'Woman at the Altar', p. 93.

5

Priestliness of the Diaconate

Deacons are called to work with the Bishop and the priests
with whom they serve as heralds of Christ's kingdom. They
are to proclaim the gospel in word and deed, as agents of
God's purposes of love. They are to serve the community
in which they are set, bringing to the Church the needs and
hopes of all the people. They are to work with their fellow
members in searching out the poor and weak, the sick and
lonely and those who are oppressed and powerless, reaching
into the forgotten corners of the world, that the love of God
may be made visible.[1]

The particular calling to the ministry of deacon is essential to
the life of the Church. Among denominations that recognize
a distinctive ordained ministry of deacons, deacons are commonly overlooked. They tend to be subject to comparison with
the particular calling to ordained priesthood and are often
defined by the particular acts that are not part of their ministry, rather than by the particular shape of the ministry to
which they have been called and which is essential in building
an anti-clericalist Church. Deacons are normally associated
with ministries of service. We shall see below that recently the
association of deacons with acts of humble service has been
challenged and a renewed emphasis placed on the particular
commissioning of deacons to certain tasks in the life of the
Church.

In the liturgy in the Western tradition, they introduce the
congregational act of confession, proclaim the gospel, prepare
the gifts of bread and wine for the celebration of the Eucharist,

administer the chalice at communion, do the washing-up (more technically, the ablutions) and send people on their way (more technically, the dismissal). We see in the introduction to confession and the dismissal that the deacon is a kind of go-between. However, this particular ministry is often over-looked, even in churches and denominations that celebrate the threefold order of deacon, priest and bishop.

The overlooking of the particular ministry of deacons is almost certainly due to a particular kind of clericalism – the association of 'priesthood' with 'leadership', and the propensity to collapse general talk of vocation into the particular call-ing to the ordained ministry of priest. A church that in *theory* recognizes the ordained ministry of the deacon but in *practice* discerns and nurtures relatively few callings to the particular ministry of deacon is a church that is likely to be experiencing this kind of clericalism.

While of course God is free to call hundreds to the priest-hood and relatively few to the ministry of deacon, any church that holds to the threefold order of ministry but that is experi-encing an imbalance in the numbers called to the priesthood and the numbers called to serve as deacons must ask itself whether this is a result of God's will or because of clericalist structures and processions of vocation operating within that church. This is especially so because the ministry of deacons is a vital contribution to overcoming clericalism in every church, as we shall argue in this chapter.

Deacons remain relatively rare compared to those who are called to the ordained ministry of priesthood. In the Church of England, however, there is no priest who hasn't served at least some time as a deacon. In common with many other denomin-ations who had retained the so-called threefold order of ministry (deacons, priests and bishops) the Church of England does not ordain to the priesthood candidates unless they have first been ordained deacon for a period of time. Those ordained deacon with the intention of later being ordained priest are known as 'transitional deacons'. Those ordained deacon because that is the particular calling they have discerned and the Church has recognized are sometimes called 'permanent' or, better, 'distinctive' deacons.

While this transitional period of serving as deacon is often thought to remind those ordained priest that their ministry is always 'diaconal' (a term we will come to below), in fact this can end up having the opposite effect. Those called to the particular ministry of priest can feel that since they too have been ordained deacon, but have been elevated to a higher status and calling, they already know or ignore the insights of those whose particular calling to diaconal ministry is essential to the life of the Church, and the ministry of an anti-clericalist Church. The term 'diaconal', as we shall see, often has associations with certain kinds of service and humility. Indeed, the ministry of many permanent deacons is marked by such acts of humble service. However, we must be alert to the power dynamics of such language. The association of 'leadership' with priesthood and 'service' with the diaconate enables a certain kind of power relation between the orders of ministry to be maintained.

We argued above that ordained priesthood was about a particular calling in association with the priestly acts of celebrating the Eucharist and reconciling through proclaiming absolution on those who have fallen out of fellowship with a particular community, rather than a particularly elevated call to status or position within the Church. Here we shall see that the ministry of deacon also has a eucharistic element – the call to repentance of life, the proclamation of the gospel to the people, a ministry of preparation at the altar, a ministry of 'sending out' – but that these eucharistic acts are not defining in the same way as celebration and absolution are for the particular call to priesthood. Rather, for the deacon, these roles in worship reflect the particular call of the deacon. This call is a call to the margins, a commissioned ministry to the margins so that the centre of church life may always be upset by the margins and that the various processes of marginalization that occur in the life of the Church can be held to account through the ministry of deacon. In this respect, the deacon's role in eucharistic liturgies of dismissal (sending the gathered congregation once again to the margins) and introduction to confession (inviting congregational repentance for the ways in which they have remained close to the centre or participated in new and existing forms of marginalization) are given their proper significance.

In what follows I will refer to the ordained ministry of 'deacon' without the qualifier of 'distinctive' or 'transitional'. I prefer to do so as it makes the particular calling to the ministry of deacon primary. This reflects clearly that the ministry of deacon is the primary calling to ordained ministry. Rather than defining the ministry of the deacon by what it is not – 'Deacons are like priests but can't absolve, celebrate the Eucharist and so on but they get to wear shirts with funny collars' – we shall instead define the particular calls to ordained ministry as primarily calls to share in the ministry of those called to exercise the ministry of dwelling in the margins and holding the centre to account. This is the ministry of the deacon. Priests are then ordained to particular acts within the body of Christ – the celebration of the Eucharist and the pronouncement of reconciliation – and bishops to oversee and administer the discerning of the particularity of various callings (lay and ordained) across the whole of the Church. The commonplace 'once a deacon, always a deacon' may hold true but this is because of the universal call to the margins, not because the ministry of deacon is one that is so easily surpassed.

It should be apparent that the particular call of the deacon, not only to the margins, but to hold the centre and processes of marginalization to account (through introduction to confession for the processes of sin and marginalization, the proclamation of the gospel, sending out once again to those currently marginalized) is essential to overcoming clericalism within the Church. It should also be apparent that the relative lack of attention paid to the diaconate in the Church is perhaps unsurprising as it will perpetually require the centre to be open to acknowledging its own complicity in the processes of marginalization. Rather than a form of ordained ministry that is reserved for those who are seen as lacking some aspect that qualifies them for the priesthood (as has been the case for women called to ordained ministry in the Church of England, or those called to marriage and ordained ministry in the Roman Catholic Church), the particular calling to the diaconate is a call to the margins and a particular calling to hold the processes of marginalization to account.

The diaconate and Christ's priesthood

We saw the ordained priesthood has the potential to resist clericalism when it is grounded in Christ's unlikely and unexpected priesthood. If this pattern of Christ's unexpected, expansive, unifying, faithful pattern of Christ's priesthood and the dramatic renunciation that is at the heart of Christ's supreme priestly act in the Last Supper, and with which those called to serve as priests are particularly associated, is at the fore of ordained priesthood, it is an essential tool in keeping the focus on Christ and preventing the clericalist diminishing of the particularity of vocation to which individuals are called. The ordained ministry of priest is associated with Christ's priestly dramatic renunciation at the Last Supper in a particular way. Those called to celebrate the Eucharist are called to the particular act of presiding at this communal celebration of Christ's dramatic renunciation. The call of the deacon is not unrelated to this priestly renunciation, however, their role is distinct. The deacon folds the edges into the eucharistic heart of the Church.

There is an essential 'priestliness' to this act. Just as the cultic priests of the Old Testament were seen as mediating figures between God or gods and humankind, the deacon is also a kind of mediator. The deacon mediates between the centre of church life and the margins of existence.

Although, as Paula Gooder notes, 'at no point in this narrative is Jesus' act described as diaconal: *diakonos* and its cognates simply do not occur in this passage', the washing of the disciples' feet by Jesus in John 13 is often seen as the diaconal act *par excellence*.[2] Walter Kasper finds in the foot-washing the very origins of the diaconate:

Therefore, at the Last Supper, on the evening before his suffering and his death, he not only established the idea of priesthood, but, in principle, also laid the foundation of the diaconal ministry. By the washing of feet he gave us an example, so that we also do, as he did to us (John 13:15). In these words one can see the foundation of the diaconate.[3]

It's significant that in the evening we see Christ's priestly act of renunciation in the Last Supper that Kasper also sees the foundation of the particular calling to the ministry of deacon. We saw above that Nicholas Perrin recognized in the washing of the disciples' feet a kind of priestly consecration akin to the ritual cleansing required by priests before entering sacred space.[4] These insights point towards what is sometimes called the unity of ordained ministry.

Ordained ministry – whether deacon, priest or bishop – shares in the events of the Last Supper in particular and distinct ways. Ordained ministry is a sharing in Christ's priesthood in a particular way. It is not a greater or lesser share of Christ's priesthood than other and lay ministries, although it is distinct. Each of the three particular callings to ordained ministry is itself distinct in relation to Christ's priesthood: an episcopal ministry of oversight intended to discern and release the particular callings of the whole Church, a priestly ministry of eucharistic celebration and reconciliation intended to enable an ever greater focus on Christ and a share in his dramatic priestly renunciation in the Last Supper, and the diaconal ministry of mediation and recentralization of the margins.

These three ministries provide a particular order to the Church that, when exercised in conjunction with one another and, vitally, with the myriad of lay callings to particular ministries in the Church, offer the means of overcoming clericalism in the Church: an oversight that enables and releases, a priesthood that is for ever re-enacting the priestly renunciation of Christ at the Last Supper, a diaconate calling the margins to the centre and holding the centre to account, and a myriad of lay callings ever being nourished by this oversight of flourishing, eucharistic reconciliation and diaconal attention.

It's important in recognizing the fundamental priestliness of the diaconate that we avoid a common clericalist step here (one that as a person called to the particular ministry of ordained priesthood I am aware that I am all too likely to fall into). This is the potential for those ordained priest, having once been ordained deacon, to identify and appropriate all that is good in the diaconate and to take the distinctive calling to the diaconate on ourselves. The recognition of the priestliness of the diaconate in the sense outlined here is only useful in so far as it illuminates the importance and distinctiveness of the particular call to serve as deacon. Likewise, saying that all priestly and ordained ministry is primarily diaconal, in the sense that it must be attentive to the margins and the process of marginalization, can also serve to undermine the centrality of a vital and vibrant diaconate to a church that is anti-clericalist to its core.

I think it's helpful here to consider the agency of the ministry of deacon that is assumed in the theology of the diaconate set out here. We shall see this in greater detail when we come to look at the nature of *diakonia* in Scripture. For now, it's worth noting that the kind of diaconate we are articulating here is an 'active' one. It is active in dwelling in the margins, overcoming marginalization, and folding in those who find themselves at the edge. Often, however, 'diaconal' can be used in a passive or self-emptying sense associated with humility and acts of service or simply as emissary to those ordained bishop or priest. An active priestly leadership can be contrasted with a passive diaconal servanthood. There is, of course, an activity and passivity to both callings. Just as Christ is both priest and victim in the Last Supper and crucifixion, so too the dramatic priestly renunciation to which his actions at the Last Supper point and the diaconal ministry of service we are exploring contain both active and passive elements.

Yet, in identifying ordained priesthood more primarily with the priestly renunciation in the Last Supper and identifying the ordained diaconate more primarily with the ministry of Christ in acts such as foot-washing (especially John 13.15: 'you also should do as I have done to you') we are reversing what might be thought of as the usual descriptions of activity and passivity in these orders of ministry. This reversal is akin to the kind of reversal that Sarah Coakley identified as occurring in the celebration of the Eucharist facing east, particularly by a female celebrant.[5] This reversal helps to overcome the potential for clericalism in seeing the particular calling to ordained priesthood as the primary vocation in the Christian life.

Moreover, as we come to explore the use of the term *diakonia* in the New Testament, we shall see that its association with a commission or 'being sent' might imply that the ministry of deacon relies upon the ministry of priests and bishops to do the sending. We shall see that the deacon's calling, while exercised in service of the whole Church including bishops and priests, is primarily in response to God's calling rather than an episcopal or presbyteral commission. The deacon's sending out of people at the end of the liturgy, which is a traditional diaconal role, is a sending in its own right and a reflection of their own sending to the margins. Just as they have been sent and send out, so we in the deacon's dismissal in the liturgy are sent and called to send and receive others.

Diakonia

Traditionally, the ministry of deacon has been associated with acts of humble service. The Greek for deacon is *diakonos*. It is related to the term for 'ministry' (*diakonia*). It is therefore sometimes unclear whether the term *diakonia* refers generally to ministry or to the particular ministry of a deacon as such. As Paula Gooder notes: '*Diakon-* words have produced in English two distinct words: deacons and diaconal ministry on the one hand and "ministry" on the other. The former refers to a distinct ecclesial role; the latter can refer (though does not always do so) to a general description of activity within and by the church.'[6] For example, the term denotes a variety of particular ministries at 1 Corinthians 12.5 ('there are varieties of services [*diakoniōn*], but the same Lord'). Elsewhere it may denote a more general sense of ministry such as in 1 Timothy 1.12 where the author uses the term to describe his particular calling 'to his service' (*diakonian*), though even here the term denotes the particularity of the calling of the author. Later in the same letter the term *diakonos* seems to be used more precisely of a deacon: 'deacons [*diakonous*] likewise must be serious, not double-tongued, not indulging in much wine, not greedy for money' (1 Timothy 3.8). That there is a clear relation (and creative tension) between ministry in general and the particular calling to the ministry of deacon underlines the vitality of the ministry of deacons in the Church.

There has been a transformation in how to translate these terms which has emerged in recent scholarship through the work of John N. Collins. Collins has argued persuasively that the translation of *diakon-* words such as *diakonos* (deacon) and *diakonia* in terms that suggest menial or humble service is a misreading of the original sense of the term. We find such an association of deacons with these acts of service in the ordination of deacons service in the Church of England. Deacons are 'to serve the community in which they are set ... in serving [others, deacons] are serving Christ himself'.[7] Likewise, the World Council of Churches' document *Baptism, Eucharist, and Ministry* emphasizes this service:

> Deacons represent to the Church its calling as servant in the world. By struggling in Christ's name with the myriad needs of societies and persons, deacons exemplify the interdependence of worship and service in the Church's life ... They exercise a ministry of love within the community.[8]

Collins argues instead that the *diakon-* terms should be translated to reflect that the primary sense of these terms concerns the commissioning of an individual on behalf of another:

Because the root idea expressed by the words is that of the go-between, the words do not necessarily involve the idea of 'humble activity' at all, and never express the idea of being 'at the service of' one's fellow man with what that phrase implies of benevolence; in commonly signifying that an action is done for someone, the words do not speak of benefit either to the person authorising the action or to the recipient of the action but of an action done in the name of another. This, which also applies to actions done in the service of God, means that the words do not speak directly of 'attitude' like 'lowliness' but express concepts about undertakings for another, be that God or man, master or friend.[9]

Collins recognizes that the use of the *diakon-* word group in the Gospels does include commissioned tasks which 'mainly designate menial attendance of one kind of another'.[10] We can see this in the use of the term for the attendants at the wedding at Cana (John 2.5, 9) or in the parable of the marriage feast to describe the king's servants (Matthew 22.13), where the term is clearly used as a synonym for slave (*doulos*) (Matthew 22.3, 4, 6, 8, 10). Collins's point, however, is that this is not necessarily so. Rather, a commission on behalf of another is the primary and defining feature of a deacon in particular and *diakonia* generally.[11] We can see this sense of the term reflected in the earliest witnesses to the role of the deacon in the early Church. Liturgically we can see this in the role ascribed to the deacon by Justin Martyr (*c.* AD 105–65). In his *First Apology*, written in the middle of the second century, Justin describes the role of the deacon in the liturgy in terms that reflect this sense of being commissioned on behalf of another, in this case the presiding presbyter in the eucharistic liturgy. The deacons administer communion on behalf of the presiding presbyter to those present and to those absent through, for example, sickness.[12] Justin demonstrates the relationship of the deacon acting on behalf of the presbyter in this case. Ignatius of Antioch (*c.* AD 35?–*c.* 107?), writing either a generation before or shortly after Justin, demonstrates this sense of 'deacon as commissioned' theologically and with respect to the bishop:

> while your bishop presides in the place of God, and your presbyters in the place of the assembly of the apostles, along with your deacons, who are most dear to me, and are entrusted with the ministry of Jesus Christ, who was with the Father before the beginning of time, and in the end was revealed.[13]

Ignatius implies here a parallel between the relationship between deacons and their bishops and the sending of the Son by the Father in the Trinity. Collins argues: 'the axis of the analogy here is Father–Jesus, which expresses the idea that as Jesus did the will of the Father the deacon does the will of the bishop. Jesus could well have been called the "deacon" of the Father'.[14]

Collins's fresh interpretation of the *diakon-* word group in Scripture and the early Church is convincing. However, it has not gone unchallenged. Part of the resistance to accepting Collins's refocusing our attention on the commissioned nature of diaconal ministry has been that it might loosen the connection between the ministry of deacon and the kind of loving-service that has been associated with *diakonia*. Moreover, the loosening of the tie between the diaconate and the language of service reminds us that there are many more particular callings that incorporate such commissions to loving service than the call to serve as deacon alone. Gooder recognizes the benefits of this observation: 'the role of the deacon, or minister, is instead associated with the carrying out of a commissioned task, a task commissioned by the Church, bishop or, indeed, God. What is important about this is that it allows for greater reflection about the specificity of a deacon's role without removing from all baptized Christians the role – indeed requirement – of humble, loving care for one's neighbour.'[15]

Collins notes that there is no reason why the commissioned set of tasks that are particular to the deacon could not on occasion include such acts of service too. There is, however, an understandable sense of loss that this form of service does not categorize all the commissioned tasks of the deacon. The Latin American bishops at Puebla in 1979 set forth the advantages of such an understanding for the Church as a whole: 'the charism of the diaconate, a sacramental sign of "Christ the servant", is very effective in bringing about a poor, servant Church that exercises its missionary function for the integral liberation of the human being'.[16] However, the sense of deacon as commissioned has advantages over the language of service, as we noted above, because such menial service language can all too often be used to render the deacon passive.

This might at first seem to be the case for the commissioned deacon too. The deacon is passive in relation to the active commissioning bishop or presbyter. The potential clericalist abuse of this power relation is overcome when we regard the deacon as commissioned not *by* the bishop or presbyter but *into relationship with* the bishops and presbyters as part of their particular calling and commission *by* God. As Paula Gooder notes in a detailed reflection on Collins's work, 'We must be very clear that adopting this view does not mean that we abandon humble care for our neighbour; rather, that we focus more on why we do it. The primary reason for caring for our neighbour is doing what God requires.'[17]

Furthermore, the destination of this commission to the margins in order for the margins to be ever related to the centre (through the deacons to the bishops, priests, and those in leadership positions within the Church or local Christian community) is itself also an aid to overcoming the potential for clericalist abuse of the deacon's commission to service.

A second ground of criticism has emerged in the light of Collins's interpretation of diaconal ministry as commissioned task. This is because the commission to a particular set of tasks raises questions for the increasing tendency for *diakonia* to be translated as the 'ministry' in general which belongs to the whole Church, rather than the particular ministry of those called to the particular calling of deacon. We can see both senses of the term operating with scriptural texts and the earliest Christian witness. It is not so much that ministry includes particular tasks that has been the grounds of criticism, but that such an understanding of the *diakonia* and related words implies a ministry of particular service by particular people (and, we would argue, to those particular margins that are the product of whatever system of marginalization is current in the Church of the day).

Collins is strident in his criticism of the modern tendency to describe all Christian discipleship as 'ministry' and to apply the term '*diakonia*' to all callings lay or ordained. He argues that such a tendency trivializes the biblical witness to the specificity of calling and task that is implied by *diakonia*.[18] Collins's reassessment of the language of *diakonia* helps us to restore to this vital ministry a sense of the specificity involved in the diaconate as a whole. It also helps to recognize the particularity of all callings which has been a constant feature of our exploration. As Gooder notes: 'ministry is more to do with the carrying out of a commissioned task than it is about care of one's neighbour, that the model of humble service while a vital element in Christian tradition is not solely tied up with *diakonia*, and that more general ministry, as a result, can have the more specific focus of commissioned or mandated tasks than it is often given in the modern church'.[19]

The particular calling of the deacon

This specificity of calling to which Collins's reassessment of *diakonia* alerts us reminds us of the particularity of all calling. It also, however, alerts us to the particular calling of the diaconate in the Church, the commission to the margins by which deacons serve God and the priests and bishops with which they are in fellowship. Deacons are those with a particular commission of God through the bishop to act as the kind of go-betweens between the margins and the centre that we saw is implied by the term and the ancient role of deacon in the liturgy and early Christian community. In a modern sense this requires not only a commission to the margins but an attentiveness to the processes of marginalization that create new forms of margin and marginalized people. This diaconal commission and attentiveness are essential to overcoming clericalism within the Church, especially the clericalist tendency to promote and highlight particular callings, people and elites within the Christian life. The ministry of the deacon is essential in alerting the Church to such clericalism and in holding the centres of power in church life to account.

In this sense too we discover the relationship between Christ's priesthood and the ministry of deacon. Paula Gooder notes how Collins's reassessment of the term *'diakonos'* widens the set of terms in the New Testament with which the ministry of deacon is associated:

> consequently *diakonos* begins to have meanings in common with *apostolos* (messenger) and even *presbeuo* (to be an ambassador). One end of the spectrum emphasizes the menial aspect of *diakonos*, whereas the *apostolos* end emphasizes its representative function. In fact, the two ends of the spectrum are not as far apart as they might appear, for both ends emphasize the fact that the *diakonos* serves the master – whether as a slave at table or as an ambassador on a mission.[20]

This diaconal commissioning demonstrates the particular calling of deacon in the Church in those who are to 'go between' the margins and the centre, and to perennially draw those who are marginalized in current ways of being and 'doing church' into the centre of the Church's life. The term *'diakonos'* is a synonym of the term *'therapōn'* which appears as 'servant' at Hebrews 3.5, and from which we get one of our biblical words for healing (*therapeúō*). For a Church that has been healed from the scourge of clericalism, we can say that a vibrant ordained diaconate will play the role for which it has been commissioned by God. Deacons will play their particular part in being sent by God through the bishop to the margins, and thereby encounter and overcome the forms of marginalization present in the Church and society, of which clericalism is one form. We now turn to another much more pernicious form of marginalization, the sin of racism, and consider how a church that is anti-clericalist will be a church with anti-racism at its heart.

Notes

1 The Archbishops' Council, *Common Worship: Ordination Services* (London: Church House Publishing, 2007), available at: www. churchofengland.org/prayer-and-worship/worship-texts-and-resources/ common-worship/ministry/common-worship-ordination-0 [accessed 22. 06.2014].

2 Paula Gooder, '*Diakonia* in the New Testament: A Dialogue with John N. Collins', *Ecclesiology* 3.1 (2006), pp. 33–56 (p. 50).

3 Walter Kasper, 'The Deacon Offers an Ecclesiological View of the Present Day Challenges in the Church and Society: Paper presented at the International Diaconate Centre Study Conference, Brixen, Italy, October 1997', 2.2, available at: https://clergy.org.au/diaconate/ item/the-ecclesiological-view-offered-by-the-deacon-2 [accessed 23.09. 2021].

4 Nicholas Perrin, 'Jesus as Priest in the Gospels', *The Southern Baptist Journal of Theology* 22.2 (2018), p. 91.

5 Sarah Coakley, 'The Woman at the Altar: Cosmological Disturbance or Gender Subversion?', *Anglican Theological Review* 86.1 (2004), pp. 75–93.

6 Gooder, '*Diakonia*', p. 56.

7 Archbishops' Council, *Ordination Services*.

8 *Baptism, Eucharist, and Ministry* (Geneva: World Council of Churches, 1982), p. 31, available at: www.anglicancommunion.org/ media/102580/lima_document.pdf [accessed 17.09.2021].

9 John N. Collins, *Diakonia: Re-interpreting the Ancient Sources* (Oxford: Oxford University Press, 1990), p. 194.

10 Collins, *Diakonia*, p. 245.

11 See also Gooder, '*Diakonia*', pp. 44–5: 'If this reading is correct, then the governing understanding of the *diakon-* words is the undertaking of a task or mandate commissioned by someone else. This shift of perspective cannot help but affect our view of service. It turns it from being a description of looking after one's neighbour to the fulfilling of a task on behalf of someone else.'

12 Justin Martyr, *First Apology* 65, 67, available at: www.new advent.org/fathers/0126.htm [accessed 25.09.2021].

13 Ignatius of Antioch, *Magnesians* 6.1, available at: www.new advent.org/fathers/0105.htm; cf. *Trallians* 3.1, available at: www.new advent.org/fathers/0106.htm [both accessed 25.09.2021].

14 Collins, *Diakonia*, p. 240.

15 Gooder, '*Diakonia*', p. 54.

16 Final Document of the Third General Conference of the Latin American Episcopate, Puebla 1979, 697 in J. Eagleson and P. Scharper (eds), *Puebla and Beyond* (Maryknoll, NY: Orbis Books, 1979), p. 219, cited in Collins, *Diakonia*, p. 42.

17 Gooder, '*Diakonia*', p. 42.

18 Collins, *Diakonia*, p. 259.

19 Gooder, '*Diakonia*', p. 56.

20 Gooder, '*Diakonia*', p. 48.

6

Anti-clericalism and Anti-racism: A Test Case for an Anti-clericalist Church

Unless the status attributed to being white is examined, the white historic church will continue both consciously and unconsciously to limit the voice, action and influence of her own non-white members, her women, her members of the queer community, her neuro-diverse, and those who live with disabilities. (A. D. A. France-Williams[1])

If clericalism is the elevation of certain models, vocations, or ways of 'being church' in such a way as to diminish others, it should be clear that there are substantial overlaps here with the mechanics of racism. Just as racism elevates certain characteristics (typically whiteness) and particular people (typically white), so clericalism elevates certain characteristics, callings and people within the Church.

Racism is a form of idolatry: the deliberate or unintentional setting apart of particular peoples and groups, the unacknowledged privilege of particular people or groups over others which is present within our worship and the life of the Church as a whole.

Scripture's persistent warning against idolatry is a reminder that to maintain our focus on God and that which God intends requires constant attention, vigilance and interrogation of those attitudes and assumptions at work in our worship and in the life of the Church.[2] Deuteronomy 6 underlines the need for constant formation in order to keep the love of God at the heart of our life and worship and not the particular peoples and groups that look and sound like us which we are tempted to elevate if left to our own devices:

> Keep these words that I am commanding you today in your heart. Recite them to your children and talk about them when you are at home and when you are away, when you lie down and when you rise. Bind them as a sign on your hand, fix them as an emblem on your forehead, and write them on the doorposts of your house and on your gates. (Deuteronomy 6.6–9)

Racism is at root an issue of power, the limiting of the capacity of certain people and groups to act while privileging and promoting the capacity of others, solely on the grounds of racial characterization. Even our worship and the life of the Church are not free from these dynamics.

Racism is a negative force for those who are marginalized consciously or subconsciously by those who are knowingly or unknowingly elevated and who benefit from the systems and behaviours that reinforce systemic racism. A. D. A. France-Williams notes that for those who are marginalized through racism, the hallmarks of existence in a world and Church that favour whiteness are 'mini assaults on one's personhood' which 'are death by a thousand paper cuts'.[3]

Clericalism, as we have said above, is also bad for those who seemingly benefit from it, whereas the disparities caused by racism are so large (and the benefits accrued by those who obtain privilege from the processes of marginalization that keep systemic racism afloat) that the same cannot be said of racism. Put simply, there are parallels between clericalism and racism in that both elevate particular people and characteristics. These parallels cease in that the elevation of whiteness over non-whiteness exists to benefit those who are white at the expense of those who lack the privilege of whiteness.

To describe 'white privilege' is likely to make some readers feel vulnerable. As a white man, I'm personally aware of the feelings of vulnerability and fragility that discussions of racism can invoke. Reni Eddo-Lodge describes the potential reactions that discussion of racism can invoke from 'bewilderment and defensiveness'[4] to 'dull, grinding complacency'.[5] Ben Lindsay notes that these reactions can categorize responses to racism within white-majority churches, highlighting that 'the shortness of empathy and lack of responsiveness from some white Christians ... maintains racial inequality in the Church'.[6]

To use the term 'white privilege' is not to say that all white people enjoy white privilege or that all white people benefit from white privilege to the same degree. There are other forms of marginalization and discrimination at work which prevent the benefit of white privilege from being felt in the lives of white women (who experience the marginalization of misogyny), white LGBTQIA+ people (who experience various forms of marginalization including trans-, homo-, and bi-phobia), white people who are living in poverty or from working-class backgrounds (who experience the marginalization of prejudice against the economically poor and working class), those who are discriminated against on account of their mental health, and so on and so on. Often people who experience these other forms of discrimination and marginalization are prevented on other grounds from accessing the kind of spaces in which white privilege is most keenly felt.

Racism takes a number of forms. There is the xenophobia expressed towards particular white communities who are denigrated for not truly belonging, such as that expressed towards people of Eastern European background. There is the particular form of racism that is antisemitism which, unlike most other forms of racism denigrating those categorized as belonging to a particular 'race', perversely accentuates Jewish people in order to present Jewish people as a threatening force within society.[7] There are forms of anti-black racism that are the legacy of the systemic societal attitudes that were needed to enforce the system of slavery. This legacy, France-Williams notes, is the antichrist whose regeneration leaves death in its wake. It no longer lives on through its creators ... the contagions of transatlantic slavery infected institutions with anti-black racist ideologies to justify selling black humans for their own interests and profit ... the ongoing legacy of the genocidal transatlantic slavery beats on, and this sickness, unless addressed will end in death.[8]

These forms of racism do not always exist in isolation. Eric K. Ward has described the relationship between anti-black racism and antisemitism that exists within white supremacism.[9]

Racism forms a test case for a truly anti-clericalist Church. A Church that is truly anti-clericalist will be a Church that is at the forefront of overcoming racism in Church and society. Through its intentional focus on the particular callings of individuals it will call out racialized characterizations and abuses of power. Through the exercise of its ministry to enable the flourishing of all people, an anti-clericalist Church will enable an anti-racist Church to be less of a distant dream and more of a realized goal. Anti-clericalism, and in particular an anti-clericalist priesthood and diaconate, are an essential part of building a bridge to a truly anti-racist future.

Anti-clericalism, and the priesthood and diaconate exercised in the intentional ways in which we have begun to set out, along with the genuine flourishing of the full particularity of callings that such exercise of ministry enables, will prevent the potential for certain models of power that assume whiteness. More especially, it will prevent the tendency for white models of power to organize the Church and society in the interests of preserving whiteness' capacity to act. At times, this self-preservation can take the form of the promotion of representation or visibility of those who are not white not entirely for their sake and flourishing but for the sake of, or through the benevolence of, whoever happens to be in a more significant position of power or status. All too often this fails to recognize that much of the hierarchy of the Church is not a safe space for those who lack the particular characteristics that are functionally, if not publicly, esteemed. France-Williams describes the 'white male sun which is a centre-point of a shared known universe ... no matter the benevolence of the captain, the brutality inscribed in the ship's design compromises the power of the captain to be good'.[10]

Even benevolence leaves the capacity to act and the lived experience of those who are racialized different as a whole largely untouched. This is not just limited to issues of racism. The same dynamic can be observed with respect to gender, sexuality, class and so on. Such self-preservation operates at the expense of the more difficult and costly work of enabling a Church and society in which those with the particular characteristics previously or currently valued are more easily able to flourish, while the calling and capacity of others who lack such characteristics are diminished in their capacity to live life in all its fullness and the particular calling for which God has created them. As France-Williams notes, 'Black and brown people are not asking for white protectors, but they are asking for partners who see, hear and speak up for the full human flourishing of black and brown people ... White people who speak up, listen up and look up.'[11]

There are parallels here between certain forms of clericalism and whiteness. Willie James Jennings in his exploration of the role of whiteness in current models of theological education sets outs to describe what he calls the myth of 'white self-sufficient masculinity'.[12] Clericalist patterns of church that are focused only on promoting the interests and vocation of clergy or new forms of lay elite also operate with a model of self-sufficient existence. The particularity of calling to flourishing around these forms of elite is ignored as if these forms of elite priestly or lay leadership are not also diminished through the distortion of their own calling in a clericalist Church.

The importance of anti-clericalism here is that to be anti-clericalist requires an attention to the mechanisms of clericalism that favour particular peoples, callings and characteristics over others in the way we live and serve as the Church. The particularity of calling embodied in the variety of callings including the particular callings to episcopacy, priesthood and diaconate are therefore vital in alerting the Church to where particularity of vocation is being overlooked at the expense of the promotion of generalized characteristics or peoples or groups. It is for these reasons that an anti-clericalist Church will be a Church better suited to the task of anti-racism that lies ahead.

A Church that is anti-racist is alert to these forms of racism, their interrelationship and the practices and societal attitudes that sustain them. Love Sechrest notes that,

> while the word 'race' is common in antiquity, the ancients do not generally tether the concept to observations about skin colour or physical traits as is done in the modern context … the age of European colonialism in the sixteenth through eighteenth centuries produced a discourse about race that focussed on the simple 'fact' of distinct races.[13]

A Church that is anti-racist embodies Keith Kahn-Harris's observation that 'to adopt the term anti-racist is to subvert the idea that "races" exist, while still recognising the existence of prejudice based on a belief that races exist'.[14]

To be a Church that is truly anti-racist requires more than simply the visibility of those who do not seem to share visible characteristics of whiteness. To be a Church that is truly anti-racist requires intentionality to dismantle the attitudes and practices that currently privilege whiteness and also requires an honest reflection on how power is held at every level in church life. It is here where anti-clericalism and anti-racism overlap. A Church that is anti-clericalist is better able to become a Church that is anti-racist. A Church that is anti-clericalist is more alert to the processes of marginalization and discrimination. To be anti-racist is to call out the myth that 'races' exist while recognizing the lived experience of those who suffer from the process of being racialized in society, in order that all people may truly flourish and exercise their potential and capacity to act.

A chosen race, a royal priesthood, a holy nation[15]

In the concept of priesthood we found in the pages of the New Testament above, we saw that the New Testament applied the concept of priesthood primarily to Christ and to Christians only in a corporate sense. The imagery of priesthood while appropriate to those ordained 'presbyter' is a later application flowing from Christ's primary priesthood.

In the context of this chapter, it's important to note that there is a 'racial' element to this language of corporate priesthood, which is also an important element in the Church's commitment to anti-racism. It also points further towards how particular ministries (lay and ordained) function after the priesthood of Christ to enable the particular vocation of all believers. Guido de Graaff in an article on the 'priesthood of all believers' traces the potential political ramifications of the concept and the potential for 'sacrificial civic action ... that is politically transformative'.[16] However, we can go further in exploring how New Testament language of Christ's priesthood and corporate priesthood here entails a commitment to anti-racism. This in turn shapes the exercise of ordained priesthood as we encountered above, grounded on Christ's unlikely priesthood.

We saw above that Christ's priesthood was unexpected because he was born outside of the Aaronic and Levitical descent that was the expected source of priestly identity. The application of the language of priesthood to Christians as a whole draws upon terms that help point towards an anti-racist exercise of Christian ministry modelled on Christ's own priesthood. Christ's priesthood points us towards the importance of anti-racism in its being located out of the usual and expected lines of family descent. Christ's priesthood, arising out of a family descent that is usually marked off from priestly ministry, raises questions for the legitimacy of such familial descent being the grounds for the potential exercise of ministry. With respect to the later institution of ordained and other ministries via the laying on of hands we see that baptism – a new birth – is the ground for the exercise of such ministry. Familial descent or nationality is replaced by incorporation into Christ as the sole grounds of identity from which all ministry emerges. There is no particular characteristic beyond this that serves to favour one person over another in the fulfilment of the particular calling God has placed on their lives.

We see this further in how the language of priesthood is applied corporately to Christians in the New Testament. The corporate application of the language of priesthood to Christians in Revelation 1.6 and 5.10 refers to a 'kingdom of priests' (echoing the use of the term in Exodus 19.5–6). The use of this term to apply to all Christians points towards the kind of anti-racist space the Church is called upon to become. Both times the phrase is used in Revelation it is in close association with the death of Christ through which this kingdom of priests is established. While Revelation does not draw directly upon the 'holy nation' motif of Exodus here (which we see echoed in 1 Peter below), there is a reference to nationality here or, rather, nationality is transcended in this royal priesthood. The Christian royal priesthood is established through Christ's blood which 'ransomed for God saints from every tribe and language and people and nation' (Revelation 5.9).

1 Peter 2.9 maintains the theme of a 'holy nation' from Exodus 19: 'you are a chosen race, a royal priesthood, a holy nation, God's own people'. However, it is important to see how the Christian use of this theme differs from the use of the images in Exodus. It is not simply the case that a Christian supranational priestliness replaces a Jewish holiness limited to the people of Israel alone. Such a reading is open to the long history of Christian antisemitism. Rather, the holiness of the nation in Exodus 19.5 is based on the people of Israel's obedience to God and their faithfulness to the covenant that they have been gifted by God. The Christian use of this term is based not on this particular covenantal relationship but on Christ's death on the one hand and the shared worship that this death inspires and enables on the other. To draw on our

earlier analysis, if the holiness of the people of Israel is based on their faithfulness to the covenant gifted to them, the holiness of the Christian community is based on their faithfulness to Christ's act of priestly renunciation at the Last Supper. Such a renunciation includes a renunciation of the nationalistic and tribal groupings that mark all human society. It also involves a renunciation of the process of creating new tribes and racialized characterizations that has served to promote the interests of those who share one set of characteristics (typically white, straight, maleness) at the expense of those who do not.[17]

In 'racial' terms such a renunciation is a familiar theme in the New Testament, especially in the writings of Paul. Paul's writings on what God has done in Christ often reflect the overcoming of the racial divide between Jews and Greeks. So, for example, in Galatians 3.28 we read that 'there is no longer Jew or Greek ... for all of you are one in Christ Jesus'. Similarly, in Colossians 3, we read that in the new creation 'there is no longer Greek and Jew, circumcised and uncircumcised, barbarian, Scythian, slave and free; but Christ is all and in all!' (Colossians 3.11). Participation in Christ trumps any national, ethnic or racial characteristic or identity. Paul often reflects the re-prioritizing of ethnic identity in relation to Christ. In Philippians 3, he writes how his new relation to Christ subverts previous privilege which may have been afforded by his nationality or ethnic or racial characteristics: 'If anyone else has reason to be confident in the flesh, I have more: circumcised on the eighth day, a member of the people of Israel, of the tribe of Benjamin, a Hebrew born of Hebrews; as to the law, a Pharisee; as to zeal, a persecutor of the church; as to righteousness under the law, blameless. Yet whatever gains I had, these I have come to regard as loss because of Christ' (Philippians 3.4b–7).

Caution is needed here. In a Church in which preference is afforded to particular characteristics, even unintentionally, there is a danger that the call for renunciation or subversion of all such characteristics and the prioritizing of the relation to Christ can bring further imbalance between the privilege afforded to different characteristics in society that have become reflected in the life of the Church. Love Sechrest notes that if

> power dynamic and oppression constitute the quintessence of racism in contemporary race relations ... (Paul's routine subordination of) his birth identity to his new racial identity in Christ could prove equally dangerous with reference to personal situationally selected identity if uncritically adopted by already oppressed contemporary ethno-racial groups.[18]

Sechrest's study of Paul's concept of 'race' argues that Paul in fact not only subordinates pre-Christian understandings of race and ethnicity, but he instead sees Christianity forming a new race which demands mutual interdependence of those racialized differently outside of Christ. This Christian 'race' is not simply a new superior race that is privileged over non-Christian races out of which the Church springs. Rather, it is a reformulation of the understanding of race that includes within it a recognition of the interdependence of those previously identified as belonging to other racial groups. Sechrest again reminds us that in the contemporary Church there is a danger that the consequences of living as this 'new race' and recognizing interdependence can be differently felt. She suggests that this might include groups who are not currently racialized perhaps needing to acknowledge this lack of racialization in public discourse even as they embrace membership of the new Christian 'race': 'interdependence and mutuality requires that whites live in a way that eschews an "unmarked" status and visibly adopt a lifestyle that marks them as members of a distinctive race'.[19]

Sechrest's analysis of Paul also alerts us to a feature of the use of the language of 'royal priesthood' in relation to race in 1 Peter. Sechrest concludes that 'Paul's gospel renounces every attempt to normalize community relations around a set of social conventions, practices, behaviors, or appearances that belong to the powerful' and implies 'a racial construction of Christian identity that embraces powerlessness and exile along with the transformation of racial and ethnic birth identity that occurs in Christ'.[20] This requires, as Sechrest notes, that Christians both renounce 'the bonds of allegiance to birth identity even as they preserve the memory of having been born Gentiles who were "aliens from the commonwealth of Israel and strangers to the covenants of promise" (Ephesians 2.12)'.[21]

This allows us an important insight into the use of the language of 'a chosen race, a royal priesthood, a holy nation, God's own people' (1 Peter 2.9). This language of royal priesthood is found alongside a reminder that as Christians we are 'aliens and exiles' (1 Peter 2.11). Our 'racial' identity in Christ shares in his priesthood which is itself grounded on the dramatic renunciation of the Last Supper but is also built upon a shared exilic status from all such racial and ethnic characteristics. As Church, to be God's people is not to maintain any system of preference according to certain characteristics where the characteristic 'Christian' is the new favoured or privileged group. As Church, to be God's people is grounded in the experience of being an exile from such favoured groups and the process and systems of privilege. This means that 1 Peter 2.10 takes on a new importance in our reading of the passage as a whole: 'Once you were not a people, but now you are God's people.'

As Church, rather than rest content in the privilege of belonging to a new superior Christian people group, to be God's people is to recognize a perpetual alien status from the process of favour and privilege, to be a people who carry alive the memory of the priestly act of renunciation at the Last Supper which constitutes our formation as those who remember that as a people group they are a 'once you were not a' people group. A Church in which this dual process of renunciation and acknowledgement of exile and the refusal to embrace new patterns of marginalization and favour is to become an anti-clericalist Church. This renunciation and recognition of exile enables us to look outside those tribes and groups we might expect to discern particular callings as it alerts us to the processes of favour and privilege that condition us to see vocations to ordained, lay, or other particular ministries to be found among particular sets of characteristics or ways of life. Such a Church requires the constant focus on Christ and intentionality of ministry that we uncovered in the liturgical traditions associated with the celebration of the Eucharist in the Western tradition.

In such a Church, the ordained priesthood is a particular ministry associated with presidency at the celebration of the Eucharist and the memory of that evening of dramatic priestly renunciation, which keeps this renunciation at the fore. In such a Church, the ordained diaconate is a ministry to the margins, to keep alive our memory of perpetually exiled status as Christians, to fold the margins to the centre, and to resist all forms of marginalization that occur, especially those that occur from a Christian amnesia that we are called to be exiles to the creation of powerful groups and favoured characteristics. In such a Church, the particular people who inhabit all the multiplicity of Christian callings will be enabled to flourish as the Church as a whole will be genuinely attentive to God's will and resist the patterns of tribalism that tend to identify particular kinds of people as favoured for leadership rather than the more scandalous particularity of God's call.

An anti-clericalist Church

To be anti-clericalist in this way enables the whole Church to flourish and enables all individuals to flourish according to the particularity of their calling. Such a Church requires not the abolition of the priesthood and the diaconate but rather the exercise of the ordained priesthood and diaconate according to the particularity of those callings. An ordained priesthood grounded on Christ's unlikely priesthood, intentional in its focus on Christ and its searching for those whom God is calling to ordained ministry. Such a priesthood is alert to the potential for ordained priesthood to become reflective of the particular groups and peoples who are privileged in the Church and society. Christ's unlikely priesthood – outside of the expected or privileged priestly tribe of his day – reminds us to be attentive to the callings to ministry generally and to ordained ministry in particular among those who are unexpected in the current pattern of church life. An ordained diaconate is commissioned with a particular task to be alert to the systems and patterns of marginalization. Ordained deacons commissioned to ensure that the centre of church life is never unaware of life at the margins of society but in close proximity to them, and that those who are being marginalized by the way we are existing as Church are returned to the 'centre'.

A Church in which those called to the particular ordained ministries of the priesthood and diaconate are released and able to flourish in the particularity of that calling will be a Church in which those callings to ordained ministry are not elevated in status above the multiplicity of lay callings that make up the Church of God. A Church that is anti-clericalist will not elevate or ascribe status to certain (ordained) callings but will elevate the particularity of calling as such. Priests will be priests, deacons will be deacons, and the multiplicity of callings will be enabled *through* the exercise of these ministries and others. This requires the greater intentionality, which we have been tracing in this book, in how the ordained ministries are lived out because of the potential for their elevation on the one hand and the potential for a clericalizing generalization of vocation or the setting up of new lay elites on the other – both of which in effect diminish the capacity of others through a reduction in the particularity of vocation. An anti-clericalist Church therefore requires a more intentional exercise of the particular ministries of priesthood, the diaconate, and essentially a greater intentionality in enabling the particular callings that make up the multiplicity of gifts and callings across the whole of God's Church.

Notes

1 A. D. A. France-Williams, *Ghost Ship: Institutional Racism and the Church of England* (London: SCM Press, 2020), p. 8.

2 See Stephen E. Fowl, *Idolatry* (Waco, TX: Baylor University Press, 2019), for the argument that constant catechesis is needed to overcome the ever-present propensity to idolatry in all its forms.

3 France-Williams, *Ghost Ship*, p. 6.

4 Reni Eddo-Lodge, *Why I'm No Longer Talking To White People About Race* (London: Bloomsbury, 2017), p. x.

5 Eddo-Lodge, *No Longer Talking*, p. 87.

6 Ben Lindsay, *We Need To Talk About Race: Understanding the Black Experience in White-Majority Churches* (London: Bloomsbury, 2019), pp. 143, 155.

7 See Zahava Moerdler, 'Racializing Antisemitism: The Development of Racist Antisemitism and Its Current Manifestations', *Fordham International Law Journal* 40.4 (2017), pp. 1281–325, available at: https://ir.lawnet.fordham.edu/cgi/viewcontent.cgi?article=2670&context=ilj [accessed 28.09.2021].

8 France-Williams, *Ghost Ship*, p. 37.

9 Eric K. Ward, 'Skin in the Game: How Antisemitism Animates White Nationalism' (29 June 2017), available at: www.politicalresearch.org/2017/06/29/skin-in-the-game-how-antisemitism-animates-white-nationalism [accessed 27.09.2021].

10 France-Williams, *Ghost Ship*, p. xv.

11 France-Williams, *Ghost Ship*, p. 208.

12 Willie James Jennings, *After Whiteness: An Education in Belonging* (Grand Rapids, MI: Eerdmans, 2020).

13 Love Sechrest, *A Former Jew: Paul and the Dialectics of Race* (London: T & T Clark, 2009), p. 25.

14 Keith Kahn-Harris, *Strange Hate: Antisemitism, Racism, and the Limits of Diversity* (London: Repeater Books, 2019), p. 39.

15 See 1 Peter 2.9.

16 Guido de Graaff, 'Intercession as Political Ministry: Re-interpreting the Priesthood of all Believers', *Modern Theology* 32.4 (2016), p. 521

17 See Jarel Robinson-Brown, *Black, Gay, British, Christian, Queer* (London: SCM Press, 2021) for the consequences of the current ecclesial promotion of such interests.

18 Sechrest, *Former Jew*, p. 227.

19 Sechrest, *Former Jew*, p. 228.

20 Sechrest, *Former Jew*, pp. 230–1.

21 Sechrest, *Former Jew*, p. 231.

Conclusion: Unlikely Priesthood and Getting Out of the Way

We are coming to the end of our exploration of clericalism and priesthood within the life of the Church. Throughout I have been arguing that the particularity of vocation is essential to true flourishing and that the particular ministries of ordained ministry have a particular role to play in enabling such flourish. These roles are of no greater status than other ministries within the diversity of callings that make up the Church, but they are particular and distinct. A Church in which bishops, priests and deacons exercise their particular callings will be a Church in which each and every individual will be enabled to exercise their particular calling. Such a Church will be well placed to resist the clericalism of generalizing vocation in favour of certain particular callings or of generating new forms of clericalism through the elevation of new forms of elite callings or groups. A test of such a Church will be how seriously it commits to anti-racism as a pernicious form of the elevation of particular characteristics and groupings.

I turn in this last chapter to focus on how the recognition of particularity of calling may enable the flourishing of every Christian calling. I consider too how the ordained ministry (and from the experience of the author this means ordained priesthood in particular) can be exercised in such a way as to better serve the range of particularity of callings that make up the entire Church. We see that a greater focus on priesthood, especially the priesthood of Christ, can in fact liberate the particularity of calling and provide an antidote to clericalism.

However, this is so only if it is grounded on the priesthood of Christ – the unlikely priesthood which is founded on an act of dramatic self-renunciation at the Last Supper.

Burn-out

There is one hallmark of a Church that is impacted by clericalism: burn-out. A clericalist Church that neglects the particularity of calling and sets up individuals and groups as elite runs the risk of burdening even those it elevates. An anti-clericalist Church will liberate not only those who are burdened through being overlooked against the esteemed callings of individuals and groups, it will also liberate those who are burdened through such esteem. A Church that pays attention to the particularity of calling will liberate those to serve in the shape of life to which God is truly calling them.

The elevation of particular characteristics or shapes of life over others can lead to individuals either taking on tasks that are alien to the particularity of their call or that are felt as burdensome, because they are not liberated to exercise the calling to which they are being called. There is the clericalist tendency of the Church as a whole to regard only certain shapes of people as called to this or that ministry, or to over-inflate particular calls with tasks and obligations that are strictly alien to the particular calling to which the individual is called. If we are right then, for example, that the particularity of act restricted to the call to priesthood is fairly small: presiding at the Eucharist, pronouncing absolution and so on. Much of what makes up the day-to-day life of the priest, for example, is perhaps necessary for her office but it is not particular to her calling. Good governance is essential to pastoral care in a context of priestly leadership, but it is not as priest that the priestly leader recognizes that good systems of administration are an important means of pastoral care. Likewise, keeping the stage clean or tuning a musical instrument might not be in the particularity of calling to serve as a musician who leads worship, but the musician will recognize that a clean stage and a well-tuned cymbal are important in order to lead God's people in sung worship.

Clericalism distorts the particularity of call so that that which is particular to the calling, say of priest or musician, is lost among the sea of other burdens of expectation placed on the individual trying to faithfully live out that call. It is often the Church that places this clericalist burden on the individual where expectations are placed and ministries are ordered in such a way that the particularity of calling is no longer able to flourish. Indeed, the calling of those who are called to administer effectively or tune instruments accurately is also impacted by this form of clericalism. The solution to such clericalism is keener attention paid to those who God may be calling to the variety of tasks that make up church life and a mutual support in the discernment of those calls. It would be as much a clericalist Church that recognizes that a greater variety of support is needed but leaves it to the musician or the clergy person to add another task to their growing list and seek out that support for themselves. This kind of clericalism includes the placing of burden on others and asking them to do perhaps more than is necessitated to fully live out their particularity of call. Such clericalism asks individuals to do more and more and more.

However, there is another form of clericalism that is almost the opposite of this. This kind of clericalism can include an over-inflation of one's own particularity of call. This can take various forms – the elevation in status of one's own call above others or the refusal to ask for or admit the needs of others' gifts and calling in the exercise of one's own ministry. It can include a reluctance to recognize that your particular calling is that which God has called you to for your flourishing – the gift of life in all its fullness (John 10.10) – and not for the rescuing of the entire world. Such clericalism often betrays an assumption that somehow God relies on you in this calling, rather than the other way round. The sentence 'you cannot bear the weight of this calling in your own strength, but only by the grace and power of God'[1] that appears in each of the ordination services to the order of bishop, priest and deacon in the Church of England, perhaps indicates this form of clericalism is a perennial temptation for clergy.

Often such clericalism is marked by the tendency to overwork. Such over-work both involves the imposition or adoption of more than is necessary for the flourishing of your particular calling and contribute to a flourishing Christian communal life. To take on too much work clearly diminishes yourself as you become tired and approach burn-out, but it also diminishes others who are not afforded the opportunity to develop and flourish in this or that particular task to which they may be being called.[2] This form of clericalism as over-work is often reflected in our tendency to draw unhelpful parallels with God's activity *qua* God, rather than the pattern for flourishing life he calls us into in Christ and Scripture.

For example, the song 'Way Maker' includes the lyric: 'Even when I don't see it, You're working ... You never stop, You never stop working'.[3] Theologically, this song is correct. *God* never stops working. However, we are not God. We are all called to a particular calling, but none of us are called to do precisely that which God has done and is doing for us in Christ. God never stops working, but we do. We do both because of the limitations of human existence (namely our mortality) and because there are limitations to our exercise of calling that are built in to our calling as a calling that exists within the world of creaturely limitation.

If we build our expectations around how we are to exercise our calling solely in reference to God's nature and not in reference to God's nature revealed to us in Christ, we will be prone to thinking that we should be like God and never stop working. If we focus too much on God's eternal nature, we will be tempted to miss what God has done for us in Christ and think that we have to take on extra suffering for the sins of the world. Rowan Williams recounts a reminder he received on the follies of such a well-meaning but misplaced exercise of his particular vocation: 'In my middle 20s, I was an angst-ridden young man, with a lot of worries about whether I was doing enough suffering and whether I was compassionate enough. But the late, great Mother Mary Clare said to me, "You don't have to suffer for the sins of the world, darling. It's been done".'[4]

One important antidote to clericalism is the observance of Sabbath rest. Sabbath rest is both a recognition that all those who are called to a particular vocation are bound by creaturely limitation and a reminder that it does not all rest on the exercise of our particular vocation at any and all given time. To embrace a regular pattern of Sabbath rest avoids the potential for any particular individual or group to become a perpetual fixture or focus in communal life.

The necessity of such Sabbath rest in the exercise of vocation arises out of our nature as embodied creatures. We are embodied. Our bodies will fail us. We will get hungry – or hangry – and tired – and unwell. We might have a chronic condition. But it's not only those of us who are chronically ill or have a particular life-long diagnosis who have limitations. To be human is to be creaturely and to be creature is to be limited. God doesn't call us out of limitations. God calls us through them.

One of the things that the particular calling to ordained ministry as deacon, priest or bishop reminds us of is that our particular vocation arises out of our bodies. Those of us who are ordained are ordained by virtue of our bodies – the bishop's laying on of hands. There is no reason why other particular callings cannot also be inaugurated or recognized through a similar laying on of hands as a reminder that all calling to particular vocation is embodied. All vocation is the particular calling of that body. Luckily it doesn't matter how 'good' or 'bad' our bodies are. You're no lesser or greater in the exercise of your particular vocation depending on how much or little you can do, on how much or little you can exert before collapsing or how much or little you can do between burn-outs. If your vocation is to ordained ministry, you are a deacon or priest simply because that is the shape of life to which God has called you – all of you – the broken and wobbly bits along with everything else. If your vocation is to be a licensed lay minister or street pastor or youth worker or parish nurse or member of a religious community, you exercise your particular vocation simply because that is the shape of life to which God has called you – every bit of you – the broken and wobbly bits along with everything else. God calls you – all of you – broken and wobbly bits and all, even those bits regarded as broken or wobbly because they are not the bodies or shape of life expected by others within the Church.

In fact, as the Church is discerning and recognizing your call, those broken and wobbly bits are rather important. For too long as Church we've consciously or unconsciously held up images of people who are rather un-broken and rather un-wobbly. Or if they have been broken or wobbly, they have a powerful story of how Christ came crashing into their lives and un-broke them and reduced their wobble. For some of us those stories are powerful and true, but for many – perhaps most of us – we struggle to see our selves, our bodies, in the stories the Church highlights and tells.

The Church discerns and recognizes God's call in *your* life – not a younger, fitter, healthier, whiter, straighter, less complicated, more male, less broken, less wobbly version of you. *You* are created in the image of God. Sometimes the only thing that sustains you in your calling is the reminder when you look in the mirror that you are created in the image of God and called to this particular vocation. Yes, even you. The image of God is reflected in all of you. Even the broken and tired and wobbly bits.

The crucifixion, Jesus' death on the cross, is a reminder of this, but it's often a reminder we can get really quite wrong, in ways that do not help us to live the life to which we are called as people and clergy – life in all its fullness. When we see the love of God most clearly, we see it in an image of a person who has been tortured, legs broken, a human body ravaged.

Images of the cross can be used in two profoundly unhelpful ways for Christian well-being here. First, they can be whitewashed and made to look much more sanitary and pleasing. Christ is the able-bodied hero in charge of his own fate. Perhaps all the more so if we're just looking at a cross without a 'corpus', the image of Christ's bodily suffering. The message this can give is: 'Ignore what your body is telling you and neglect your own well-being. Crack on.'

Second, and in almost the opposite way, Christ's suffering can be glorified through images of the cross. Christ's suffering is held up as our yardstick to follow. The more we suffer in ministry, the closer we are to Christ. The message this can give is: 'Oh, your body is telling you that you're tired and unwell. Keep on neglecting your own well-being. You're so holy. Crack on.'

We will consider the politics implied here below, but it should be obvious that there is a power dynamic at play here, especially when we are encouraged to embrace such unhealthy images: embrace burn out, fatigue and suffering. Christ is with you.

It doesn't have to be like this. Think of the Isenheim altarpiece by Matthias Grünewald. The image of the cross here is an image that reflects the suffering of the patients at the hospital in which it was situated. Christ is presented as suffering with the same bodily limitations as the patients in the hospital. Christ is with them as they are, not in spite of their bodily limitation. The depiction of Christ's crucifixion here is not a suffering that is neglected or wrongly embraced, but a bodily limitation that's recognized and reflected in the pattern of Christian witness and ministry in that place. Such a depiction of the crucifixion reminds us that we don't need to suffer for the sins of the world: it's been done.

The importance of rest is written into the very fabric of creation in Genesis 2. Creaturely limit is hallowed in a weekly pattern of rest. The first thing to notice here is that God isn't resting *from* creation. The pattern of Sabbath is part of the work of creation God is upholding in being. This might seem a small distinction but I think it's important for how we as Christians relate to rest. Sabbath rest isn't something we do to enable a pattern of work. It's not something we squeeze in or have to look slightly embarrassed about when we put on our 'out of office' and apologize that this is our rest day. Sabbath rest is written into the very DNA of creation; Sabbath rest is part of the pattern of Christian ministry.

Importantly, God's pattern of human life shows this too. Before we move to consider Jesus' model of rest within his particular human life, I want to draw our attention to one of the hazardous lines we might be tempted to take. We see a number of times that Jesus works on the Sabbath. We need to be a bit careful here.

On the one hand, the spectre of antisemitism can make Christian readings of these passages contrast Christian Sabbath violation with a perceived Jewish legalism. The Sabbath violations are as much theological statements about who God is – just as God never stops working – so Jesus' action has an eternal element outside of the pattern of Sabbath rest of creation. We can see this in John 5 – the Sabbath violation witnesses to who we as Christians believe God to be: 'Jesus answered them, "My Father is still working, and I also am working."' He was not only breaking the Sabbath, but was also calling God his own Father, thereby making himself equal to God (John 5.17–18).

On the other hand, we can slip back into drawing our patterns of work from this eternal quality with God and be tempted to see the Sabbath violations as ending the pattern of Sabbath rest in entirety. Jesus never stops working so neither should we.

Again, there is a political element here in the images and passages we highlight and are highlighted by others to us. Sabbath violations that attest to who Jesus is are lifted up to keep us working, and passages that show to us Jesus resting, sleeping, eating, taking time to go to a family wedding, taking time out to pray and so on and so on and so on, are ignored. We see elsewhere in Matthew's Gospel that Jesus takes a time of rest after the death of John the Baptist in a time of grief (Matthew 14.13). Alternatively, we can be tempted to ignore those times when Jesus tells his disciples to rest: 'Come away to a deserted place all by yourselves and rest a while' (Mark 6.31).

If we find ourselves feeling guilty about taking a day off or a time of rest, watch what happens here in Mark 6. First, this period of rest enables a miracle. The disciples' rest in a desert place enables the feeding of the 5,000. It's the grounds for their being there. Second, watch what happens when the disciples rest: 'many saw them going and recognized them' (Mark 6.33). The 5,000 observe their rest and follow them. The patterns we set in the exercise of our particular vocation are noticed. The behaviours we model are followed. And this includes well-being and rest.

There are two more points to observe here – one theological, one social and political. Theologically, we need to be careful that we're not tricking ourselves here and that what we model is genuinely modelled on these patterns of well-being and rest: the Sabbath rest written into creation, the model of rest in God's own embrace of creaturely limitations in Jesus Christ. Once Christians have – sometimes grudgingly – admitted the need for well-being and rest, they can all too easily turn 'rest' into a work to be worked. 'I'm so good at resting'; 'Honestly, I'm ruthless at eliminating hurry and I'm just the best at self-care';[5] 'I've been on six boot camps this week alone, eight spin classes, and have managed to take ten mini-breaks in a single weekend'.

Second, there is a political element here related to what we model to those we serve. It is possible for those whose particular vocation is associated with employment by the Church or a Christian organization to model rest well and to do so in ways that don't simply reflect the kind of middle-class lifestyles that 'professional' Christianity can often bring. We can both say and model that rest and self-care and leisure and well-being are essential and written into the very being of creation and recognize that for many, if not most, such self-care and time for rest is a luxury that is currently beyond reach. Rest time is beyond us. We're run ragged by children or we can't afford time off work simply because we need the pay. As we exercise our particular vocation, we need not just to model rest, but to use our prophetic voice as Church to call for it for those we serve.

The Church in the past has lent its voice to and called for an eight-hour working day (8 hours work, 8 hours leisure, 8 hours sleep), weekends, paid holiday and so on. If rest is written into creation, we need to call out the affront to creation that is the removal of rest from the patterns of life of working people as much as we call out the affront to creation that is environmental damage. We need to not just call for this rest, but model this rest too.

All of this is easier said than done. One of the effects of clericalism is that we can find ourselves often having to ask unbelievable things of the people in our parishes and churches. We expect people to give of their time and talent in addition to working full and busy lives. This can make us feel incredibly guilty about resting when we feel *we* are depriving them of rest and recreation.

Practically, this means what we model and what we call for prophetically in social patterns of work and employment are more important not less. Yet, we also need to be realistic both about what we model and what we ask of others and ourselves. Are we asking too much of too few? Do we need to change our patterns of church or organization to better prioritize our community well-being and self-care? Are we truly being attentive to the variety and depth of God's calling to particular vocations across the whole of our community? Are we falling into clericalist patterns of expectation that this or that particular vocation can only arise in the life of that kind of person or group?

Callings of the unexpected

This is decidedly not a book that reflects on leadership in the conventional sense of the term. Language of leadership can all too easily become a clericalist endeavour in which certain ideologies, patterns of behaviour or kinds of individual are held in undue esteem in such a way as to diminish the capacity and witness of others. However, this is also decidedly not to say that the Church does not need good leaders. Good leaders are those who enable cultures and institutions in which those they serve and lead may flourish. Good leaders therefore are naturally or intentionally anti-clericalist in the way in which we have been tracing throughout. Good leadership is the exercising of one's own vocation in such a way as to be attentive to the flourishing and vocation of others and not to diminish the particular vocation of all those you are called upon to lead and serve. The argument I have been making reveals that an inevitable element of good leadership is cultivating our attention towards the unlikeliness of Christ's priesthood and grounding our relationship to Christ's priesthood in an ability to discern God's particular call in those we might think unlikely or be tempted to overlook. Stacey Abrams, the candidate for Governor of Georgia whose campaign for voter registration among black voters in the state of Georgia has been credited with achieving victory in the 2020 Presidential Election of the United States, notes the advantage of those leading from outside the mainstream and therefore beyond the pool of those clericalism esteems: 'Leadership requires the ability to engage and to create empathy for communities with disparate needs and ideas, and that's why as outsider, we can make the best and most effective leaders.'[6]

One of the travesties of clericalism is that it diminishes the flourishing of the whole Church because the particular vocations of individuals within the Church are either distorted in what it is they are permitted or expected to do, or they are completely overlooked. I have suggested that clericalist response can be to generalize vocation and that to become a truly anti-clericalist Church we need to find a renewed insistence on the particularity of a vocation. This does not mean that a variety of particular vocations can simply be assigned to various individuals or dictated to individuals by powerful groups or interests within the Church. Rather, this means a more intentional focus in the Church on the particular calling of each individual. In such a Church the particularity of all vocation is recognized and a variety of particular vocations will necessarily follow and be enabled to flourish.

One of the fruits of a recognition of the particular ministries of lay and ordained is that it enables the promotion of such particularity. It is a travesty of clericalism that leads to unequal esteem being given to vocations that happen to be ordained.

The particularity of vocation finds its origins in Christ's particular priesthood. It encourages the exercise of the ordained ministries of priest and deacon in particular ways. However, there are lessons from Christ's priesthood and from the particularity of ministry of priest and deacon that are valuable for the exercise and discernment of all Christian vocations. It is to the conclusions that can be traced from the exploration above that I now turn.

If Christ's priesthood is primary, we are alert to the fact that the one from whom all ministry extends was an unexpected and unlikely candidate for ministry. Christ was not from the expected priestly lineage and was not qualified to act as priest, let alone high priest. Yet in the New Testament we saw how Christ's priesthood is discovered and reflected upon. Christ's priestliness is seen most clearly in the events of the Last Supper in which he crucially is both victim and priest. This subverts contemporary notions of priesthood and sacrifice and means that the hallmark of the Christian life is a kind of renunciation. It is a personal renunciation that is a hallmark of priestly or pastoral ministry but it is also a renunciation of the privilege of the expected. To fulfil our particular vocation, whatever it might be, we are called upon to similar acts of renunciation. We are called to identify with Christ's suffering and death, not by taking on suffering of our own but by making *Christ's* suffering and death the hallmark of our Christian existence. As we unite our lives and the exercise of our vocation to Christ's in this way we are also called to pay attention to the ways in which we are setting up patterns of expectation. Are we falling foul of expectation and suggesting to those around us that they may be called to this or that because they fulfil our expectations of the kind of person whose vocation that might be? Or are we following the pattern of Christ's unlikely priesthood, paying attention to God's particular calling on that particular person's life to whatever particular vocation that might be? Are we open to our expectations being as confounded as those for whom Christ's priesthood was seemingly impossible on account of his birth?

Our consideration of the 'priesthood of all believers' saw Luther's attempt to write the particular pattern of clericalist abuses that were rife in his day. We saw that while the reminder that the New Testament applies the language of priesthood corporately, the term 'priesthood of all believers' was limited as a means of enabling the particularity of vocation and the flourishing of all to live the particular calling to which God has called them. We saw how the language of corporate priesthood in the New Testament extended the subversion of patterns of expectation and received characterization in terms of nationhood and physical descent that we saw in Christ's priesthood. However, we also saw how Luther's conception of the 'priesthood of all believers' was limited, as it risked homogenizing vocation by 'clericalizing' all vocation and setting ministerial priesthood as the expected form or pattern of ministry with which others compare. Instead, the creation of a newly priestly people in the New Testament use of priestly imagery corporately subverts expectations about what the very concepts of nationality and ethnicity mean and the value and esteem we place on them as markers of status between peoples. It also throws open the potential for calling beyond particular nationalities or groups and encourages us to be attentive to the call to particular vocation in each and every person no matter their background or the expectations we might be tempted to place on them.

In the call to the particular vocation that is the ordained priesthood, we saw that this particular vocation involves an intimate connection to Christ's priestly act in the Last Supper generally and in the Eucharist in particular. Rather than simply enabling clericalism, the particular exercise of the ministry of those ordained priest is vital for the potential for priestly ministry to realize its vocation as an antidote to clericalism, through its embodiment of the particularity of calling on the one hand and its refocusing, through the ministry of the Eucharist and reconciliation, on the saving acts of God in Christ. However, we recognized too that the exercise of this particular vocation is prone to clericalism when it is assumed that this is the only pattern of vocation (either to ministry generally or ordained ministry in particular). The scandalous particularity of priestly ministry only fulfils its vocation when it enables the entire people of God to be ever refocused on the saving acts of God in Christ, especially the events of the Last Supper and the night on which he died. This dual focus – on Christ's priestly renunciation at the Last Supper and on the events of the saving passion and death – forms the basis of the ordained priesthood, reflected in the particular tasks associated with this particular vocation: both in the presidency of the Eucharist, and the pronouncing absolution through the recognition of God's reconciliation of those who have sinned.

As the ministry of the ordained priesthood is associated so closely with these central acts in the life of the Church, it is obvious that the potential for clericalism was rife. However, it would be more damagingly clericalist to do away with the particular vocation to priesthood altogether because of the potential for the ministry of ordained priesthood to be exercised in such a way. Rather, what's needed is a more intentional exercise of this ministry which embraces the narrow particularity of the priestly vocation on the one hand and points people resolutely towards Christ on the other. This is achieved through its grounding primarily in Christ's priesthood, whose unexpected priestly origins serves to further save the exercise of ordained priesthood from the temptation to discern vocation to the priesthood only in those who are members of a qualifying elite or obvious and expected candidates to the particular vocation to be ordained priest.

We saw in Chapter 4 how in the Western liturgical tradition, the use of prayers that serve to focus the intention of the presiding priest on the actions of Christ help to unite the ministry of the ordained priest closely to the saving acts of God in Christ with which this particular vocation is particularly focused. However, we saw that wider awareness of these prayers was a useful means of focusing attention more firmly on Christ among all the particularity of vocations to which individual Christians are called. Moreover, they alerted us to the importance of intentionality as a means of keeping Christ squarely in focus. This resolute intentionality helps avoid the patterns of clericalism not only because our focus is on Christ, but because the same intentionality is needed in the exercise of all Christian ministry to the potential for clericalist patterns of elevation of this or that particular calling above others, or to find candidates for this or that particular vocation more likely to arise among this or that tradition or group.

A Church that is truly anti-clericalist will be a Church in which the ministry of those ordained deacon will be lively and vital. This is because this ministry is an important and commissioned 'go-between'. We saw how a fresh interpretation of the Greek word *diakonos* that lies behind the word 'deacon' suggests this ministry is a commissioned ministry rather than a ministry that is associated with tasks of menial service. Such tasks may be included in the commission but they are not essential to it. We saw that deacons are commissioned by God through the Church to be sent to the margins. They exist both to enfold those who are at the margins – through processes of marginalization that exist in the Church or in society – into the eucharistic heart of the Church. They are thus attentive to and call to account the processes of marginalization. They are also vital in overcoming the potential for clericalism in other ordained ministries, as they demonstrate in their particular vocation that the vocation to ordained priesthood is not the only vocation to ordained life. Indeed, this attentiveness to the margins and the task of calling processes of marginalization to account is an essential feature of all ministry, and ordained ministry in particular. A Church that is anti-clericalist will find all of its ordained ministries are founded on this resolute diaconal commission to the margins and to overcome whatever particular process of marginalization is taking hold in the Church of the day.

Finally, we turned to the contemporary scourge of racism as an example of one such process of marginalization. We saw that a Church that is truly anti-clericalist will be better placed to overcome the particular form of marginalization that racism is. The marginalization of those who are racialized differently from those who currently enjoy prestige in the Church (and among whom God's call to the variety of particular vocations and ministries is more readily heard) demonstrates a Church that is failing to ground its patterns of ministry firmly on Christ's priesthood. When church members who are differently racialized according to the majority are not flourishing and living life in all its fullness, it demonstrates a failure to take seriously Christ's unexpected priesthood. It also demonstrates a failure to have a flourishing ordained priesthood resolutely refocusing the communities they serve on the saving acts of God in Christ and the call to eucharistic participation, repentance and reconciliation. It also demonstrates a failure to have a flourishing ordained diaconate calling the centre to account for its failure to address the pattern of marginalization that is racism and other forms of marginalization besides. Above all it demonstrates a failure to enable the particular vocations to which God is calling each and every person, especially those who in our current systems of marginalization are not able to flourish and thrive.

Getting out of the way

The ministry of deacon is to the margins and to hold the processes of marginalization to account (and to hold the centre of church life to account where it is complicit in the process of marginalization). The ministry of those ordained priest is to refocus on Christ through eucharistic presidency and absolution, to help the Church as a whole to ever live in the upper room and at the foot of the cross which is the site of Christ's priestly renunciation, the event of our salvation and the site of our resurrection. The ministry of bishop is a ministry of oversight of these and all ministries – that is, to focus on Christ while alert to the processes of marginalization to which those exercising diaconal ministry are drawing to their attention and oversight. These particular ministries alert us to an essential feature of all Christian ministries grounded in the exercise of Christ's unexpected priesthood.

The ministry of the ordained in particular and of all Christian ministry in general is a ministry of getting out of the way. To live out a calling to any particular vocation is to commit ourselves to getting out of the way so that our shared attention is focused a little more intentionally on Christ. All particular vocations exist to enable this shared endeavour of focus on Christ which enables life in all its fullness. Life in all its fullness includes that collective 'getting out of the way' that is the Church that God is ever calling into being – a community of shared particular vocation, response and focus on Christ. A Church embodying this life in all its fullness resists the elevation of particular groups by esteem or status or privilege which is the human motivation from which clericalism takes root.

To exercise ministry in such a way that we 'get in the way' puts stumbling blocks between those we are called upon to serve. To elevate the status of a particular vocation, or to find vocations to particular ministries only because this or that person comes from this or that expected kind of person or group within the Church, is also a form of 'getting in the way'. Any form of organization or Church that puts *our* thinking, *our* system of organization, *our* idea of excellence or good leadership above the more difficult task of resolute attention to Christ and to his call in the life of each and every Christian that confounds our expectations is a form of 'getting in the way'.

Jesus' statement in John's Gospel is a challenge here: 'I am the way, and the truth, and the life. No one comes to the Father except through me' (John 14.6). We can rephrase this. No one comes to the Father through *us*. If we're tempted to think that we are the ones who are doing the calling, we are mistaken. Our role is to focus ever more attentively on Christ and the people he is calling and the vocation to which he is calling them, and to get out of the way.

To be anti-clericalist is to get out of the way. This requires a priest's celebrating the Eucharist and pronouncing absolution so that the events of the night of the Last Supper are ever more closely on the mind of the Church and those glimpses of Christ in one another and in bread and wine sustain us until we see him face to face. This requires deacons at the margins holding the centre to account so that the tasks to which God is commissioning each and every Christian may be ever more greatly realized and all that prevents marginalized communities from life in all its fullness begins to be dismantled. This even requires bishops overseeing the whole, alert to where the events of that Last Supper are not at the forefront of church life, where glimpses of Christ are difficult to see, where life is not being lived in all its fullness and new forms of marginalization are being permitted to take hold. Above all, this requires the countless and remarkable multiplicity of others *as* vital and *as* distinct callings in the lives of people who are trying in their own equally faltering ways to follow the particular call of God in their lives.

All of these callings are a call to live the particular life in all its fullness to which God is calling you and in doing so to point all people ever more clearly to the One who is the way, the truth and the life. It is through living that particular call in your life and enabling a greater ability for those around you to live the particular call to life in all its fullness which is theirs, that we all might flourish and we all might get out of the way. When such a Church is realized and we are enabled to live fully the lives and vocations to which God is calling us even now, we might well find that we are living that day in which we shall see Christ face to face.

CONCLUSION

Notes

1 The Archbishops' Council, *Common Worship: Ordination Services* (London: Church House Publishing, 2007), available at: www.churchofengland.org/prayer-and-worship/worship-texts-and-resources/common-worship/ministry/common-worship-ordination-0 [accessed 22.06.2014].

2 See Simon Cuff, *Love in Action: Catholic Social Teaching for Every Church* (London: SCM Press, 2019), pp. 88–107 for the importance of such 'subsidiarity' within human flourishing.

3 Sinach, 'Way Maker' (2015), available at: www.youtube.com/watch?v=n4XWfwLHeLM [accessed 30.09.2021].

4 Rowan Williams, in David Hare, 'Rowan Williams, God's Boxer', *The Guardian* (8 July 2011), available at: www.theguardian.com/uk/2011/jul/08/rowan-williams-interview-david-hare [accessed 30.09.2021].

5 See John Mark Comer, *The Ruthless Elimination of Hurry: How to Stay Emotionally Healthy and Spiritually Alive in the Chaos of the Modern World* (London: Hodder & Stoughton, 2019).

6 Stacey Abrams, *Lead from the Outside: How to Build Your Future and Make Real Change* (London: Picador, 2019), p. xvii.

Index of Scriptural References

Old Testament

New Testament

Index of Names and Subjects